# PHILOSOPHY OF SOCIAL SCIENCE

---

## David Braybrooke

Dalhousie University

*PRENTICE-HALL, INC.*, *Englewood Cliffs, New Jersey 07632*

**Library of Congress Cataloging-in-Publication Data**

Braybrooke, David.
  Philosophy of social science.

  (Foundations of philosophy series)
  Bibliography: p.
Includes index.
  1. Social sciences—Philosophy.   I. Title.
II. Series: Prentice-Hall foundations of philosophy
series.
H61.B639  1987        300′.1        86–9433
ISBN 0–13–663394–3

© 1987 by Prentice-Hall, Inc.
A division of Simon & Schuster
Englewood Cliffs, New Jersey 07632

Printed in the United States of America

10  9  8  7  6  5  4  3  2  1


ISBN 0-13-663394-3        01


Prentice-Hall International (UK) Limited, *London*
Prentice-Hall of Australia Pty. Limited, *Sydney*
Prentice-Hall Canada Inc., *Toronto*
Prentice-Hall Hispanoamericana, S.A., *Mexico*
Prentice-Hall of India Private Limited, *New Delhi*
Prentice-Hall of Japan, Inc., *Tokyo*
Prentice-Hall of Southeast Asia Pte. Ltd., *Singapore*
Editora Prentice-Hall do Brasil, Ltda., *Rio de Janeiro*

## MEMORIAL NOTE FOR MONROE C. BEARDSLEY (1915-1985)

One of us worked with Monroe from the start, as co-editor of the *Foundations of Philosophy* series, and remembers vividly how much his breadth of philosophic interest and his wide acquaintanceship among good philosophers did to shape the series in its formative years. His sense of style gave him a keen editorial eye, while his talent for teaching led him to suggest changes that were genuinely constructive and usually appreciated.

The other of us joined the team of *Foundations* co-editors more recently and found that Monroe's contributions to the series remained significant. Both of us feel an immeasurable loss; but we resolve that future series volumes will maintain the standards that Monroe did so much to help establish in Philosophy and in pedagogy.

| | |
|---|---|
| Elizabeth Beardsley | Tom L. Beauchamp |
| *Temple University* | *Georgetown University* |

In Memoriam

**BROOKS OTIS**

a great humanist, from whom I first
heard of Weber and of Keynes

# Contents

THREE
# Settled Social Rules on the Interpretative Side                                47

FOUR
# Critical Social Science Reduced to the Other Two                                68

# Foundations of Philosophy

Many of the problems of philosophy are of such broad relevance to human concerns, and so complex in their ramifications, that they are, in one form or another, perennially present. Though in the course of time they yield in part to philosophical inquiry, they may need to be rethought by each age in the light of its broader scientific knowledge and deepened ethical and religious experience. Better solutions are found by more refined and rigorous methods. Thus, one who approaches the study of philosophy in the hope of understanding the best of what it affords will look for both fundamental issues and contemporary achievements.

Written by a group of distinguished philosophers, the Foundations of Philosophy Series aims to exhibit some of the main problems in the various fields of philosophy as they stand at the present stage of philosophical history.

While certain fields are likely to be represented in most introductory courses in philosophy, college classes differ widely in emphasis, in method of instruction, and in rate of progress. Every instructor needs freedom to change his course as his own philosophical interests, the size and makeup of his class, and the needs of his students vary from year to year. The seventeen volumes in the Foundations of Philosophy Series—each complete in itself, but complementing the others—offer a new flexibility to the instructor, who can create his own textbook by combining several volumes as he wishes, and choose different combinations at different times. Those volumes that are not used in an introductory course will be found valuable, along with other texts or collections of readings, for the more specialized upper-level courses.

*Elizabeth Beardsley*  /  *Monroe Beardsley*  /  *Tom L. Beauchamp*
Temple University     Temple University     Georgetown University

# CHAPTER ONE

# Three Sides of Social Science

Not so long ago, there appeared in the "True Facts" section of the *National Lampoon* the following report:

A bus carrying 5 passengers was hit by a car at the corner of Sarah Street and Cook Avenue in Saint Louis, Missouri. By the time police arrived at the scene of the accident, 14 bystanders had boarded the bus and begun complaining of back injuries. All were taken to a nearby hospital.[1]

"How absurd!" we cry. An explanation of why it is absurd is hardly called for, though the explanation comes forward immediately. People are not supposed to act that way. The bystanders were not—before or after boarding the bus—in a position to attribute their back injuries to the accident. The rule is that one can make such attributions only after being causally affected by the accident in question. It is a further rule that one can move on from such a complaint to press claims for damages only when the attribution is in place. The bystanders' complaints were flagrantly out of place in two ways: first, in the attribution, which the bystanders implicitly made by raising the complaints inside the bus; second, in the claims, which we understand the attribution to be preparing for.

We may learn something from spelling these matters out carefully. However, if social science does this for us, it risks being banal, telling us little more than we already knew. It would be different if we were outsiders. Suppose we did not know about the practice of suing for damages or

---

[1]*National Lampoon* (1981): 87.

know that public transportation agencies are regarded as fair game for such litigation. We would find both the bystanders' behavior and the amusement created by the report of it very puzzling. Social science, just in helping us make sense of what was going on, could then tell us a lot that would be news to us. We are outsiders when we find ourselves dealing with exotic cultures. In another culture, perhaps, no one can get back complaints treated except by joining a group of patients collected from the site of an accident. We are also outsiders when we deal with subcultures not our own in our own society. Law courts and the legal profession constitute a subculture. Social science can tell us a lot, for example, which we could not find out by reading the laws on the books, about how litigation is actually carried on in court and on the way to court. It can tell us what outcomes to expect for various sorts of claims for damages. Would claims as baseless as those that the bystanders are preparing to press ever get a hearing in court? If not, at what stage and by what devices are they blocked?

## THREE VIEWS OF SOCIAL SCIENCE

Some philosophers incline to hold that everything that can be intelligibly and suitably attempted in social science consists wholly in bringing to light what the actions that people do signify. Social science tells us when the actions are appropriate—in place—and what expectations they give rise to. I shall call this the "interpretative" view of social science. The philosophers who hold it would not agree, nor would I, that social science so conceived is confined to explaining to us how we are to understand what is going on in cultures or subcultures not our own. They would recognize the risk of banality. They would point out, however, that there are all sorts of subtle aspects of our own actions that we probably have not reflected on closely. Just when, for example, are we prepared in ordinary life to hold some person or firm responsible for injuring another? How far does our everyday conception of responsibility match that upheld by the courts?

Interpretative questions of the sorts favored by these philosophers take us inside the bus incident and lead us to view it as the participants do. We appreciate, for example, what is in the mind of the bystanders. We thus understand their actions as virtual participants ourselves. We also participate, virtually at least, by reacting to what they do and intend to do. We laugh at it, deplore it, let it pass with tolerant amusement, or prepare to block it. Yet is this all that we might be moved to think about the incident? Are there not other questions that we could raise about it, which would not fit into the interpretative view?

There certainly seem to be. Some of them would arise for us if we were interested—on the part of the city, the bus company, or the insurance company—in keeping claims for damages within manageable limits. We would then want to find out what we could about the times and circumstances that led people to start up such far-fetched claims for damages as the bystanders, getting on the bus, were preparing to make. Are they penniless? Unemployed? Heavy gamblers who have had a run of bad luck? With these questions, we would be looking for causes of the bystanders' behavior. We would be hoping to discover, along with the causes, generalizations about the times and circumstances under which claims like the bystanders' are forthcoming. Do such claims start up less often on payday, when people feel flush with funds? More often after big games, when people have lost a lot of money in heavy betting? More often in hard times than in prosperous ones? These are questions looking for connections between statistical quantities. We might hope, however, to get beyond the statistical connections to causal generalizations asserting that whenever certain conditions were satisfied—and only then—would there be people making claims like the bystanders'.

Philosophers and social scientists (more often, as things stand, social scientists than philosophers) who think such questions constitute the agenda of social science take what I shall call the "naturalistic" view. (It is often, somewhat misleadingly, called "positivism.") If it has any room at all for the questions about rules and meaning that preoccupy the interpretative view, the naturalistic view tends to underrate them. It finds them too banal to be interesting. The naturalistic view prefers questions that according to it invite treatment by methods taken over from the natural sciences. These methods commonly begin with the observation of loose connections. They look for various conditions that make the occurrence of certain phenomena more probable. The methods in question aim to identify more perfect connections as inquiry proceeds. In the end, ideally, they look for conditions that lead without exception to the phenomena in question.

On the interpretative view, it is a mistake to try to use the methods of the natural sciences in the study of social phenomena. For just in being social such phenomena imply the presence of human intelligence, intention, and choice. One champion of the interpretative view, Charles Taylor, in a typical expression of it, holds that social science in the naturalistic tradition is impaired by "sterile" notions about methods. In consequence, and to its dire impoverishment, it "excludes a consideration of social reality as characterized by intersubjective and common meanings."[2] It is, on the interpretative view, a mistake, too, to think it even possible to have laws and theories about social phenomena comparable to those that we have for the realm of nature. Some say that it is impossible to make descriptions of social phenomena value-free. Purported scientific findings about politics will therefore always be distorted by political prejudice. Some say that it

[2]Charles Taylor, "Interpretation and the Sciences of Man," *The Review of Metaphysics* 25 (1971–1972): 3–51.

is morally wrong to degrade human beings into objects of would-be scientific study. Others say that, degrading or not, to do so is bound to belittle or ignore what is most distinctive and significant about social phenomena. It is said—and here critics resisting the use of scientific methods are joined by some critics championing those methods—there are no exact, universal laws about social phenomena, understood in the terms that currently make those phenomena significant to us. Some go on to say that there are no causal generalizations of any sort to be had with such terms.

At the very least, it may be objected that the search for causal generalizations, fruitless or not, takes us very far away from the joke about the bus incident. In the crossplay of meanings and rules lies the heart of the joke. A third view of social science takes us back toward this crossplay but raises considerations too melancholy to revive our laughter. On this view—which I shall call the "critical" view of social science—the questions to be raised about the bus incident most prominently include questions like the following: How is it that the bystanders feel so little responsibility for the public institutions of their society (if the government runs the buses and will have to pay damages)? Alternatively, if some privately owned transportation firm is involved there seems to be a breakdown in trust between the bystanders' and the firm. They are all agents and participants in market arrangements. But why are the bystanders not willing to abide by the rules of the market, which exclude force and fraud? In either case, are they alienated from their own society? Do they have cause to be, in disadvantages imposed upon them? The critical view refuses to take at face value the rules that may be cited by the interpretative view. It wants to know, whose interest is served by the rules? How do the people whose interest is served get into the position to exercise power? Through what devices does that power operate?

Many philosophers and social scientists who adopt the critical view incline to think of their view as superseding the other two. More exactly, they have so little sympathy with the naturalistic view that they incline to think of social science insofar as it answers to their view as doing a better job of what the interpretative approach begins. So the critical view, too, in its way, tends to demand exclusive rights. Which of the three views shall we choose? Many people—many social scientists—may resist choosing between them. Rightly so. Yet nothing like a systematic acknowledgment of the merits of all three views prevails. Few people, moreover, seem to realize how robust all three views are, and how complexly interconnected.

## ARE THERE THREE SIDES CORRESPONDING TO THE THREE VIEWS?

All three views will have merit if each picks out features of social science that the others disregard. To each of them, furthermore, there will then correspond some instances in social science. That they have such instances, at least potentially, has already been established, one might argue, by the differences in the three lines of questions raised about the bus incident. Yet it would be much more convincing evidence of correspondence and merit to produce actual specimens. Moreover, if such specimens are produced, one of the main things that I have to say about the three views will already be established: None of them can be granted what each tends to claim—exclusive truth.

I am about to produce three actual specimens. The naturalistic one carries out a comparison of American and Canadian political parties. The interpretative one aims to expose certain life patterns of unemployed (or underemployed) black laborers in Washington, D.C. The critical one aims to expose certain limitations of government and party competition in liberal democracies, particularly as regards policies about employment. In the course of examining these specimens, beginning in this chapter but continuing in the succeeding ones, I shall be elaborating my account of the three sides of social science that answer to the three views. (I shall revert again and again to the same specimens throughout the book. They have been chosen just because they offer such rich possibilities for comment.)

The differences between the three sides, striking at first sight, will survive this closer examination. Social scientists working on any one of the three sides will characteristically be preoccupied with different topics. They will be asking different questions in a different style and spirit. They will be pursuing different objectives. They will be seeking to give different sorts of explanations. They will be looking for different sorts of impact upon current policies and activities.

Yet as the argument proceeds, I shall be showing how these real differences coexist with a great number of parallels. On all three sides, for example, there are group facts as well as person facts, opportunities for quantitative methods, and parallel successes in meeting the standards of empirical science. I shall also be showing that there are many points of mutual dependence between the three sides. In this demonstration, I shall concentrate upon the relation between the naturalistic and interpretative sides. In methods and sorts of questions, I shall argue beforehand, the critical side of social science reduces to a mixture of methods and sorts of questions from the other two sides. The reduction leaves standing nevertheless all the important features that entitled the critical side to distinctive attention in the first place.

The naturalistic and interpretative sides are complementary in ways that go far beyond mutual support—itself remarkable—in the exchange of information. The complementarity extends to mutual presupposition between the key ideas of the two sides: causal regularities on the naturalistic side; settled social rules on the interpretative. In the end, it will become plain that the interdependence of the two sides, hence of the three, is so intimate that the three sides of social science are consistent with fundamental unity.

It is not a homogeneous unity, as in a bottleful of milk. It is a unity, but a heterogeneous one, as in a cloth woven from yarns of different textiles or (as in the case of critical social science) of different colors.


## OTHER ISSUES IN THE PHILOSOPHY OF SOCIAL SCIENCE

The book is thus organized to deal chiefly with the question, How are the three sides of social science, once recognized, related to one another? Will the book cover enough of the standard issues in the philosophy of social science to serve as an introduction to the field? It will. The chief question—the superquestion—of the book invites attention to the standard issues. They will figure in the argument as subordinate questions. A recent list of "the four major questions for the philosophy of social science" includes "(1) the cross-cultural question; (2) the humanism-scientism question; (3) the individualism-collectivism question; (4) the fact-value question."[3] The list comes from a book very different in outlook from this one, but I think it is a reasonable list. The present book will have something substantial to say about all four questions on it.

It will have most to say about the humanism-scientism question. Indeed, this question runs through the book, since the interpretative view of social science has been arrayed against the naturalistic view precisely as a means of defending humanism against scientism—that is to say, against unwarranted extensions of natural science. I shall also be treating the individualism-collectivism question in a number of passages expressly set aside for the purpose of distinguishing person facts from group facts and discussing their relations. My treatment of the fact-value questions—Can we establish facts in social science without committing ourselves on values? Should we try to?—will be concentrated in the discussion of critical social science. This is the connection in which it arises most urgently as a programmatic difference within social science. The cross-cultural question will be treated and answered in the course of recognizing that the regularities, like the settled social rules, discovered by social science may be transitory and may vary from one culture or region to another. I shall argue that discovering these regularities is a respectable scientific achievement notwithstanding; and so is discovering the rules.

The book will treat a number of standard issues somewhat more particularized than any on the list cited, among them intentionality and the distinction between reasons and causes. I do not claim that I shall be treating all standard issues. One that I shall do little more than refer to, then set

[3]Graham MacDonald and Philip Pettit, *Semantics and Social Science* (London: Routledge, 1981), 1.

aside, is the nature of functional explanations. Even a book that dispensed with an overall argument in favor of an issue-by-issue survey would inevitably omit some issues and slight others. More important, it would not offer the compensation that comes with my overall argument. Answering the superquestion about the relation of the three sides, I shall not only be offering a resolution of the most salient current controversy in the philosophy of social science, a controversy generated by the three views. I shall also, by reconciling these philosophical views to the extent that they admit of reconciliation, be giving a comprehensive philosophical account of the character of social science.

## NATURALISTIC SOCIAL SCIENCE

Producing a specimen of naturalistic social science will, as things currently stand in the philosophy of social science, create more surprise and more controversy than producing a specimen from either of the other two sides. With philosophers, naturalistic social science is quite out of fashion. But I shall bring forward my first specimen on the naturalistic side, choosing one that in overall preoccupation concerns facts quite different from those that preoccupy the interpretative view. Philosophers and social scientists who hold that view often think only of how individual persons act in the presence of others ready with the appropriate expectations to interpret the actions. They often quite ignore facts that have to do with how groups operate—groups maybe as large as nations—together with the institutions that the groups maintain.

In a famous article, Leon D. Epstein, an American political scientist, took up the problem, "Why do Canadian political parties, unlike American parties, put in disciplined and cohesive performances in the national legislature?"[4] Canadian parties in Parliament in fact vote as blocs just as British parties do. Yet in other respects Canadian politics is more like politics in the United States than it is like politics in Britain. Like the United States, Canada is a diverse nation spread out over a large land area $(F_1)$. Like the United States, it tends not to divide politically on a class or ideological basis $(F_2)$. Like the United States, it is organized constitutionally as a federal system $(F_3)$. Like the United States, it has national parties that outside the national legislature are no more than very loose federations of relatively strong state or provincial parties $(F_4)$. What Canada does have in common with Britain is the British parliamentary system $(F_5)$. Executive authority rests in a strong cabinet selected from legislators belonging to the party holding a majority in the House of Commons. It is

[4]Leon D. Epstein, "A Comparative Study of Canadian Parties," *The American Political Science Review* 58 (1964): 46–59.

this circumstance that Epstein singles out as the solution to the problem. He holds that Canadian political parties are cohesive in Parliament because they operate under the same sort of parliamentary system as the British one.

Notice how Epstein arrived at this conclusion. Beginning with the problematic feature ($F_c$, parties cohesive in the legislature) that Canada shares with Britain but not with the United States, he asks in what other respects is Canada like Britain and not like the United States? In the other respects that he considers, $F_1$, $F_2$, $F_3$, $F_4$, $F_5$, he observes that Canada is like the United States and unlike Britain in all except respect $F_5$. The respects in which there is no difference can hardly be supposed to cause Canada to be different in respect to party cohesiveness. $F_5$, however, is an eligible candidate for being a cause. In $F_5$, as in the problematic feature, Canada is like Britain rather than the United States.

This reasoning illustrates the methods outlined by J. S. Mill for identifying causes.[5] The illustration shows, moreover, that the methods admit of application, just as Mill claimed, in a case where we have no opportunity to conduct experiments. Then we must rely on sorting out observations of phenomena that take place without design and intervention on our part. Mill says, "If two or more instances of the phenomenon under investigation have only one circumstance in common, the circumstance in which alone all the instances agree is the cause (or effect) of the given phenomenon." This is the Method of Agreement, illustrated in the present case by the comparison of Canada with the United Kingdom. Mill says further,

If an instance in which the phenomenon under investigation occurs and an instance in which it does not occur have every circumstance in common save one, that one occurring only in the former, the circumstance in which alone the two instances differ is the effect, or the cause, or an indispensable part of the cause, of the phenomenon.

This is the Method of Difference, illustrated in the present case by the comparison of Canada with the United States. Since both Methods are present, we may also say that the present case illustrates the method that Mill gives third, the Joint Method of Agreement and Difference.

Now, it may be asked whether Epstein's study illustrates any of these methods very exactly. Have the circumstances been so exhaustively enumerated that we can be sure that Canada has only one circumstance (besides parties disciplined in Parliament) in common with the United Kingdom, and every circumstance save one in common with the United States? Surely not. This would be true even if, with a good test for relevance, we could

[5]John Stuart Mill, *A System of Logic*, 7th ed. (London: Longman's Green, 1868), 425–448. See also J. L. Mackie, "Mill's Methods of Induction," in *The Encyclopedia of Philosophy* (New York: Macmillan/Free Press, 1967), vol. 5, 324–332.

confine ourselves to taking relevant circumstances into account. The most that we can say is that if any of the circumstances that Epstein has taken into account is the cause of party cohesiveness, Mill's methods pick out the British parliamentary system as the only plausible candidate.

But at the very least by doing this the methods and Epstein's reasoning in accordance with them have thus led to a hypothesis about the cause worth standing by until a better one is produced. This, for an early stage of investigation, is a perfectly good scientific result. Even at the latest stage to which the investigation might be carried we would still have only a hypothesis, a statement liable to be upset when further circumstances are taken into account. Even at that latest stage, Mill's methods would apply with less than perfect exactness, because there would still be—there always will be—further circumstances.

What does Epstein's hypothesis amount to, granting that what is asserted in it may have less than a perfect claim to truth? There are three points important to note. First, it supplies a solution to the problem that was taken up, and the solution is a singular causal statement. The British parliamentary system is what causes Canada to have political parties that are cohesive in the legislature. True, the British parliamentary system is not an event. Some philosophers would use "cause" only for an event. Even they would have to grant, however, that the British parliamentary system may rank as a causal condition, and ordinary usage supports calling any causal condition a "cause." Second, like other singular causal statements, the present statement about the British parliamentary system implies a counterfactual: If Canada did not have the British parliamentary system but had the American one instead, while other things were the same, Canada would not have cohesive political parties. As a singular causal statement, moreover, it also implies a causal generalization. This is the third point. Epstein himself takes his finding to offer a lesson for any nation that wants to have cohesive political parties: Such a nation, he says, "must import more than a parliamentary system as such; it must . . . import the British . . . parliamentary system." The implication to the causal generalization emerges from an analysis of what it means to assert the singular causal statement. The British parliamentary system could not be held to be a cause in this instance if it does not in like circumstances have the same effect.

Epstein's finding—the singular causal statement about Canada—is the solution to a problem about the operation of political parties in that country. It simultaneously offers an explanation of the feature of their operation—their cohesiveness—that raised the problem. Moreover, recast, the several points consolidated in the singular causal statement offer an explanation that rests on an explicitly general premise. The causal generalization supplies this premise: Whenever a country has a British parliamentary system, it has cohesive political parties. A second premise, also an element of the singular causal statement, is that Canada has a British parliamentary system. The third element of the singular causal statement follows as the conclusion: Therefore—that is why—Canada has cohesive political parties. The deduction from the generalization may be more or less probable. If the generalization is only a probable one, the conclusion and the explanation will be only probable too.

In all these respects—in being a solution, in being a causal statement, in being connected with a generalization categorical or probable—Epstein's finding conforms to patterns found in the natural sciences. So it does, too, in the observations and reflections that went into arriving at it. Those patterns may not be found everywhere even in the natural sciences, though I think they are common. Sometimes, in the natural sciences, generalizations are not of a sort that can explain singular facts as deducible from them. They do not make those facts certain or even probable. They just say how frequently they are to be expected. Epstein has evidently got further than this. Even if he had got only so far, what he would have been doing would have been scientific.

It is true that getting as far as he has, Epstein has not got far enough to escape various doubts (which he himself alludes to). One might wonder whether "the British parliamentary system" could be completely defined independently of having cohesive parties in the legislature. One might wonder whether, insofar as they are separate facts, the system is not to some extent the effect of having the cohesive parties rather than the other way around. One might ask whether the respects in which Canada, the United States, and Britain had been compared included all the respects that might be causally important. One might contend that, as a rather rough and ready finding, the finding and any generalizations that it implies are likely to be superseded by a more refined analysis.

A more refined analysis might, among other things, make more explicit the relation between the condition of having the British parliamentary system and other conditions that combine with it to produce cohesive political parties. Epstein is not entirely clear about whether he has identified a sufficient condition or a necessary condition or a condition both necessary and sufficient for having cohesive political parties. This lack of clarity is typical of causal thinking. It arises from the ways, which I shall discuss in the next chapter, in which the idea of a necessary condition and the idea of a sufficient condition both enter into the ordinary notion of a cause. A more refined analysis of the kind that I am alluding to would specify in an acceptably complete way just what sorts of conditions are involved and just how they are related.

One might have doubts about whether this could be done easily or even, in the face of the inevitable looseness of Mill's methods, whether there is any good criterion for achieving it. These doubts, however, should not be allowed to discredit gains in knowledge just because—inevitably—the knowledge gained is imperfect. They do not, any more than the others mentioned a moment ago, put Epstein's work outside the sphere of science. Solutions, causal statements, generalizations (laws, or at least what are offered as laws), and explanations throughout science are subject to just these sorts of doubts. They cannot be laid to rest completely, putting solutions and findings out of the reach of all future attempts to discredit them. If they did not run risks in these respects, they would not be doing the job that empirical science assigns them. Only statements that risk being falsified can fix upon the features that make our world what it is rather than what it might possibly otherwise be.

Nevertheless, we should try to preserve the gains of earlier stages as we move on to more advanced and refined ones. We may also properly ask that anything offered as a solution to a problem about phenomena be defensible in ways appropriate to the stage of refinement that inquiry about the problem has reached. Only then will we have a good case for preserving the solution by introducing qualifications at the next stage. In the present case such qualifications might restrict the general causal law implied by Epstein's finding to a class of societies that were prepared to have, not just the form of the British parliamentary system, but also vigorous party competition.

Epstein can and does successfully defend his work by the standard of being defensible at the stage of refinement reached when he carried it out. The respects in which he compares the three countries are all respects that students of politics regard as important ones. Hence, the list is not an arbitrary one, even if, as we must recognize, those students are fallible. Epstein considers respects that I have not mentioned, such as the prevalence of single-member, simple-plurality elections, which, he points out, holds for all three countries. As such, this would be ruled out as an eligible cause by Mill's methods. Epstein has several answers to the doubt about causal priority. One of them is the historical fact that the practice of having the cabinet retain office only so long as a majority in the legislature supports it preceded the development of cohesive parties.

## INTERPRETATIVE SOCIAL SCIENCE

Sharply contrasting in methods with the overall cast of Epstein's study are studies in social science that manifestly answer to the interpretative view. Such studies characteristically contrast with Epstein's also in the sorts of facts that they make most prominent. A good deal of social science—and it may be so far the most successful part of social science—is preoccupied with the actions of individual people. It asks of these actions, What do they signify for the people who do them and at the same time for the people who react to them in appropriate ways? When we are dealing with actions within our own culture, we already know, before any professional students of society come onto the scene, a lot of the answers to this question. However, we had to learn those answers in the course of becoming full participants in the culture. When we were just starting out as infants we did not know them.

When we turn to a different culture, most of the answers have to be discovered. The answers that work in our culture will not do. Moreover, even in our own culture, there are many specialized fields where actions are intelligible only to people initiated in them. Consider the procedures of the courts, for example. There are subcultures that even more strikingly fall into pockets of variation from the main culture: Mennonites, other religious communities, circus and carnival people. There are aspects even of familiar actions intelligible throughout the main culture that we impart to them or react to without being able to identify or explain in the absence of systematic inquiry. Just what is conveyed by a person's folding his arms? It is only a beginning to recognize that it is not something we do when we are asking a friend for a favor.

In *Tally's Corner,* a book about unemployed and intermittently employed black men in Washington, D.C., Elliott Liebow, an anthropologist, undertakes to show how those men make sense of their situation and accordingly act as they do.[6] Why do they feel less commitment to their jobs, and even to having jobs at all, than people elsewhere in American society? Liebow's answer, abundantly illustrated from what these black men say, is, in part, that the jobs pay too little for them to support their families. The jobs are, to boot, menial jobs which neither the men themselves nor other people much respect. Why do they fail to make prudent provisions for the future, blowing a week's pay in a weekend binge? Liebow says that it is not because they are less future-oriented than people who do make prudent provisions. It is because—with good reason—when they look to the future they find it hopeless. Why are their relations with women so difficult, most troubled when the women's children are their own and the men are living with the women and children in more or less formally constituted households? It is, Liebow asserts, because then their inadequacy as family providers, hence as heads of families, is most inescapably evident and most painful.

Prominent—I think justifiably prominent—in accounts of interpretative social science is the notion of rules and rule following. I am going to interpret the patterns of behavior that Liebow describes in terms of rules. Let us recognize at the outset, however, that the interpretative view is as much interested in intention, choice, and meaning as in rules. For many—perhaps most—champions of interpretative social science, rules are interesting less for their own sake than for the light that they throw upon

[6]Elliott Liebow, *Tally's Corner* (Boston: Little, Brown, 1967).

these other matters. Champions of interpretative social science incline also to be specially interested in the personal and idiosyncratic—in what sets off one person and one choice from other cases. Here, perhaps unwittingly, they tend to move outside social science, which even on the interpretative side is interested in repeated phenomena—the typical—to join up with the interests that people take in biography, the novel, and poetry. An important motivation at work in the interpretative view, in fact, may be a concern that social science should not develop in such a way as to frustrate those interests.

I wholeheartedly share this concern. Yet the typical has its own interest. Attention to the typical, on the interpretative side of social science, leads us to rules. It does not lead us to rules alone. Not everything about the repeated patterns of behavior that Liebow describes is a matter of conforming to rules. The men on Tally's Corner are, in part, reacting to what Liebow calls "objective factors," like the scarcity of jobs or the discrepancy between their income and the demands on it. Their reactions may fall under rules (though they may not). But the objective factors mentioned are not themselves rules, even if they are to some extent effects of rule following. Moreover, much of what the men do is best represented not as conforming to but as failing to conform to rules. The men on Tally's Corner, like the bystanders climbing onto the bus, do not act according to rules that other people conform to. Their actions demonstrate what is as true of rules as is typical conformity—that people, even under rules, retain a personal capacity to deviate from them, even, like the bystanders, to abuse them. They also retain, as we shall see in due course, a collective capacity to rescind the rules or simply to allow them to fall into disuse.

The men on Tally's Corner depart from certain rules. Their actions might be understood as such departures, with rules cited to explain what they were departures from, if the actions were idiosyncratic. In this case, the actions are not idiosyncratic. They are, on Liebow's account, typical of what the men on Tally's Corner do. Alternative rules creep in to take the place of the rules that are flouted. The flouted rules, together with standing rules that the men do not flout, continually make their presence felt, however. They contribute essentially to defining the possibilities of action and to giving actions their significance. Accordingly, Liebow's study of what the men do is continually concerned with what rules they are conforming to or flouting. In this it is typical of the interpretative side of social science.

The contribution that rules make to defining the possibilities of action is equally a contribution to explaining the actions actually taken. In the simplest case, the actions conform to prevailing rules: A man seeks a job and makes every effort to keep it. Having a steady job is the only respectable way for him to gain the income required to support a family. He marries and undertakes thereby not only to abide by the rules of marriage, including the rule that he should support his wife and children. By marrying, he also conforms to rules according to which a man signifies that he has the capacity to provide this support—to be a regular provider. He will cite some of these rules in giving reasons for what he does. Other rules will be cited by observers as making explicit in one way or another how the actions are understood by the agents who do them and by other people in their milieu. These rules, too, as soon as they are recognized as such, are logically suited to being invoked as reasons for doing the actions.

Three points need to be made right away about explanations that deal in reasons and conformity to rules.

First, they are solutions to problems, just as naturalistic explanations are. One has a problem about why, at the outset of their working lives, the men on Tally's Corner go to such lengths to find and keep jobs, when later their commitment to having jobs is so loose and fitful. The solution includes the point that in the beginning the men are trying hard to conform to the rules by which they can establish themselves as regular providers. I do not mean to say that the problem to which this is a solution is not in important ways different from problems that get naturalistic solutions. Problems that get naturalistic solutions do not, for instance, focus attention on what people are trying to do. Nor do the solutions anticipated or actually brought forward. To put this difference in the standard terms, the naturalistic side is concerned with "behavior" rather than with "action."

Nevertheless the sorts of solutions also have a number of things in common. Among them—and this is the second point that I wish to make at this juncture—is the fact that the solution in the interpretative case as well as in the naturalistic one can function as an explanation, represented in a more or less tight argument. In the simplest case, the rule under which an action falls can be cited as the major premise of the argument, with the minor premise asserting that the conditions or circumstances envisaged in the rule obtain. Thus there is a rule according to which a husband and father must seek a job to provide regularly for his family. Such and such a man is a husband and father. Therefore, he must seek a job. Will he actually seek it? The argument just given is, at least when cast in the first person, an instance of a practical syllogism. It concludes with a prescription that may or may not be followed. However, if the man in question does not in fact seek a job, his failure to act is at least inapposite. It is not, like seeking a job, what one would expect from knowing that he accepted the premises.

My third present point is that, solution or explanation, Liebow's findings are empirical ones, which stand or fall with observation. This is as characteristic of interpretative social science as anything else about it. Liebow could not have said what rules the men on Tally's Corner lived by if he had not observed them closely for quite a long time. Furthermore, anything that he does say about such rules is subject to upset by further observations. So what he says, like what Epstein says, runs the risk of falsification.

The story about rules on Tally's Corner is more complicated than the story in the simplest case. The men would conform to the rules about marriage and providing for their families if they could, but they cannot. They begin by trying, but they discover that steady jobs, which pay them enough for them to be regular providers, are not available to them. So they fall into a habit of decrying marriage as a trap, which men enter only under coercion. They go further: They set up alternative rules. Professing adherence to those rules, they claim that the only right way to treat women is to exploit them for all they've got. It turns out—because the men are human beings, who are susceptible to forming attachments—that they can no more live up to this counterideal than they can realize the ideal of respectable family life.

Clearly this is not a simple story about conformity to rules. It is not even a simple story about flouting them, another possibility of action defined by the rules that otherwise would have been conformed to. Besides rules, "objective factors," like the scarcity of decent jobs, enter. So do the reactions and attitudes of the people involved, as they try to adapt to their difficulties and interpret them consistently with carrying on their lives on the lines open to them. Yet rules are in the picture throughout. The men on Tally's Corner act the way they do in order to retain as much self-respect as possible. The grounds on which they can get respect, and thus have self-respect, are supplied by rules. One rule is if you cannot have respect as a regular provider, then you must at least get it as someone who ruthlessly makes as much as possible of his opportunities. That rule figures importantly in the interpretation that the men on Tally's Corner give to their relations with women. It would not be difficult to represent all their reactions and attitudes as involving rules of interpretation.

## CRITICAL SOCIAL SCIENCE

Will we find rules and interpretation or regularities and causal explanations in specimens of critical social science? I shall argue, in due course, that we find both. This advance notice is enough to suggest what is in fact true, that the claim of critical social science to occupy a third, different side of social science has a different footing from the claim to distinctiveness of the other two sides. Before we compare these claims, however, we need to have an illustrative specimen of critical social science before us. I shall not, however, as I have for naturalistic and interpretative social science, bring forward a specific, widely acclaimed study that it has produced.

Such specimens can be found. In a later chapter I shall produce one from a French writer. None that I have come across, unfortunately, including that one, quite makes the contribution to the unity of this book and its argument that we need. We need a specimen that is general enough in its concerns to stand for a broad range of the varied and disputatious literature that I mean to cover under the head of "critical social science." It should also be a specimen that links up directly with the examples from Epstein and Liebow by treating themes that are prominent, some with the one author, some with the other. It should treat, in particular, the proceedings of national legislatures (Congress or Parliament) and unemployment or underemployment. To get such a specimen I shall construct one, guided by the German philosopher Juergen Habermas's discussion of the two themes in his book *The Legitimation Crisis*. [7] The specimen thus constructed will show at once what critical social science makes of topics treated on the other sides of social science and in particular how it would treat—criticize—the treatments given those topics by Epstein and Liebow.

My specimen and my account of critical social science in this chapter will be simplified as well as constructed for my specific purpose. The two themes in the specimen have been prominent in the Marxist critique of ideology, which is a prototype of critical social science and in particular of the critical social theory put forward by the Frankfurt School new (a group of German thinkers of which Habermas is the most prominent figure) and old (an earlier German group of which Herbert Marcuse [1898–1979] was the member who became best known in the English-speaking world). [8] Contrary to some deliverances of critical social theory, I hold that the critique with these themes is topical still.

On the theme of proceedings in national legislatures, the blunt and unqualified assertion of the critique is that the opposition of liberal and conservative parties (in the United States, of Democrats and Republicans) in the national legislatures of bourgeois states is a sham so far as issues go. None of these parties is going to take any position on issues that threatens the interests of the property-owning social classes. At most, the parties disagree about what policies will currently be most effective in serving those interests. (Of course, they also disagree on who should hold the jobs, in the legislature and elsewhere in the government, that invent such policies and carry them out.) Consequently, the agenda of national policies, in the legislature and in the elections through which the legislature is composed, is everywhere, under capitalism, strictly limited. Fundamental issues about class structure and the distribution of income are not seriously discussed, much less resolved.

In particular, the agenda is limited in respect to unemployment, which brings us to the second theme to which I apply the Marxist critique of ideology. Unemployment is not, of course, something that the property-owning classes suffer from directly. It is something that falls directly upon

[7]Juergen Habermas, *The Legitimation Crisis*, trans. Thomas A. McCarthy (Boston: Beacon Press, 1975).

[8]Marcuse's *One-Dimensional Man* (Boston: Beacon Press, 1964), a representative work, will be drawn on in chapter 4. Other prominent figures in the old Frankfurt School, which began its work at the beginning of the 1930s, were Max Horkheimer (1895–1973) and Theodor W. Adorno (1903–1969).

those who have no property in the means of production—the working class, or proletariat. It is, however, something of an embarrassment for the property-owning classes and bourgeois political parties. They have, however, a way of laying the embarrassment to rest, which satisfies them and indeed misleads many or most of the victims of unemployment, even for generations on end. The way is this: Something presenting itself as social science argues that extraordinarily high unemployment occurs from time to time because wages are not flexible enough and workers are not mobile enough to allow the market to work out perfectly in allocating them to jobs. Sometimes high unemployment has to be accepted as an inevitable incident of policies combating inflation. It is held that the inflation that has to be combated came about in the first place because wages pushed up beyond the level that a perfect market would have arrived at.

The Marxist critique of ideology holds that this so-called social science is in fact an ideological mystification. The scientists concerned share with the general population, and in particular with the privileged classes, the assumption that the current system is basically the best that can be contrived. Anything, for example, that is lost with unemployment will be more than offset by what everybody gains during periods of general prosperity. Similarly, any jobs lost from instituting free international trade will be more than made up for. The market makes the most of the resources and technology currently available—a better most the freer it is to operate. The market also offers an optimum procedure for digesting changes in technology. For those who believe these things, no force or threats are required to keep the agenda of politics limited. It would seem idle to almost everybody concerned to ask whether unemployment, for example, could be eliminated under some other sort of social system. On this point and on other important ones, the agenda is limited by general consent, resting on an ideological consensus.

With these themes in hand, the critique of ideology would comment on Epstein's work that at best his finding was trivial. Disciplined or undisciplined, the parties in the Canadian Parliament would do nothing, except perhaps by mistake, that would not serve the capitalist class. At worst, the finding distracts people from inquiring into matters that are not on the agenda, including the question how various features of the system operate to limit the agenda short of dealing fully with unemployment. The critique of ideology would be inclined to say of other works on party competition and party discipline that they assist in rationalizing the current system by intimating that the form that parties take and what they do is of fundamental importance. Sometimes critique should resist this inclination. Epstein himself specifically disavows any implication that the cohesiveness of Canadian political parties, as contrasted with the indiscipline of the American ones, makes any great difference to the issues taken up in Canada or the adequacy with which the issues are treated.

Marxist critique might take a somewhat more favorable view of Liebow's study. In the eyes of the critique, Liebow has several methodological virtues. One consists of showing how under the pressure of economic circumstances people shift from one set of rules to another and with the shift change from one subjective conception of their lives to another. Liebow also has the virtue, both theoretical and practical, of relating his finding about the difficulty that the men on Tally's Corner have in living up to the rules of respectable society to the fundamental structural weakness of the system in which they live—that is, its incapacity to provide satisfactory steady employment for everybody. However, the critique of ideology would condemn Liebow for not going on to make the crucial point that this weakness is not something that has to be put up with as an incident of an imperfect, but generally beneficial, market. Nor is it something that practical measures remedying the imperfections of the market can be expected to eliminate.

In the eyes of the Marxist critique, it is crucial that everybody concerned— social scientists as well as the people under study—be brought to understand that alternative social arrangements are available that would assure everybody of a decent job. Those arrangements would achieve other good things too, including a more defensible distribution of income. Understanding this prepares people to choose things that they did not realize were available for choice. As rational agents, given the chance, they would choose other arrangements because they would thereby improve their lives. They are thus, subjectively at least, in the way in which they are brought to understand their present situation, emancipated from the limits previously imposed on their conception of society and politics.

The thought of being emancipated by bringing things—ideas, conceptions—out into the open that are not only hidden but that strongly resist discovery suggests that something like the techniques of Freudian psychoanalysis would be apposite. Some inheritors of the Marxist tradition— the Frankfurt School in particular—have been more than willing to make use of Freud's ideas, especially since Marx's straightforward program of dissolving ideology by revolutionary advances in social science has seemed to them too simple. Yet the basic notions of hidden truths and of resistance to their discovery are already present in Marx's theories of ideology and alienation. Alienated in different ways from the real process of production, both workers and intellectuals are subject to ideological delusions. Intellectuals in particular live by elaborating, in the name of science, ideological constructions that disguise uncomfortable, embarrassing, and removable features of current institutions. The constructions reinforce the self-deception to which the workers, like other inhabitants of the system, are prone anyway by giving it the backing of spurious scientific authority.

The critique of ideology is perfectly ready to acknowledge its concern with emancipation. Indeed, it advances the concern as the chief of its virtues in making social science relevant to fundamental social issues. It has little use for the notion of "value-free" social science. If the values are the right ones, like the concern with emancipation, their presence is nothing to be embarrassed about. When they are the wrong ones—assisting in the ideological defense of an oppressive social system—the claim to be "value-free" turns out to be, characteristically, a device for mystifying people, hiding the presence and operation of values that should be questioned.

# CHAPTER TWO

# Causal Regularities on the Naturalistic Side

How far can accomplishments on these three sides of social science reach? Among philosophers, the naturalistic side has been besieged during the last quarter century with objections that purport to set narrow limits for accomplishments there—limits so narrow as to give only vanishing room for any accomplishments at all. One philosopher, Karl Otto Apel, representing the interpretative side and the critical side at the same time, rather grudgingly accepts some "limiting cases" of social science on the naturalistic model: mathematical linguistics; certain studies of consumers' behavior. He comments, however, disparagingly, that these "quasi-nomological behavioral sciences" exist "only by a certain denaturization of the characteristic structure of the historical process of human society" and by isolating research from full communication with the people whose behavior is being studied.[1]

The objections alluded to earlier go on arising: Efforts in the naturalistic perspective to discover causal regularities have been fruitless. Causal explanations are out of place. If causal explanations could be had, they would lend themselves to systematic abuse by sinister interests eager to manipulate masses of people as mere objects.

Is the example from Epstein, with its chief results, then spurious? On the contrary. Causal questions like those that Epstein raises are characteristic of innumerable studies in social science. There is no substitute for

[1]Karl Otto Apel, "Types of Social Science in the Light of Human Cognitive Interests," in *Philosophical Disputes in the Social Sciences*, ed. S. C. Brown (Brighton, Sussex: Harvester Press, 1979), 22.

such questions. They are, like all causal questions, questions about regularities. The answers to them, though loose, accord with the most sophisticated current analyses of causation. The answers, moreover, like the questions, have some minimal quantitative implications. Characteristically, both lend themselves to quantitative development beyond this minimum. They also lend themselves to formal treatment in other ways, especially in the elaboration of axiomatized empirical theories. Even in Epstein's relatively simple case they rank relatively high on a scale of scientific achievement. They do so, moreover, without having to break away from the concepts of ordinary language to more rigorous concepts defined especially for scientific purposes.

## THE COVERING LAW MODEL OF EXPLANATION

Epstein's explanation of the presence of cohesive political parties in the national legislature of Canada by Canada's having the British parliamentary system is a causal explanation. Fully set forth, a causal explanation makes the causal law or regularity on which it depends explicit and presents it as one of the premises in an argument of a certain form. The form is one that has been held (by Karl R. Popper, Carl G. Hempel, and other contemporary philosophers of science) to be the basic form of scientific explanation and one in which social science properly emulates natural science.[2] It is often called "the covering law model of explanation." What is to be explained is exhibited as something that in the circumstances the law covers and implies.

The law premise of such an argument is a universally quantified proposition. It asserts that if a number of specified conditions ($C_1$, $C_2$, $C_3$, etc.) are met, then any object or system (something "$x$" not yet named or identified) that meets those conditions will have a certain further property—call it "$F$"—distinct from any of the conditions. In Epstein's finding, we could regard having the British parliamentary system as representing a combination of more specific conditions. More conveniently for present purposes, we may regard it as one condition that Epstein is tacitly assuming to be accompanied by a number of others if it is to have the effect of there being cohesive parties. If it is $C_1$, then $C_2$ might be that there is not so much commotion and confusion at the time of taking a vote in Parliament as to prevent members from discovering how the party leaders

[2]Karl R. Popper, *The Logic of Scientific Discovery* (London: Hutchinson, 1959 [originally published in German, 1934]), 59–62; Popper, *The Poverty of Historicism*, 2nd ed. (London: Routledge, 1960), 122–124; Carl G. Hempel, *Philosophy of Natural Science* (Englewood Cliffs, N.J.: Prentice-Hall, 1966), 49ff. (cf. Hempel's essay, originally written in collaboration with Paul Oppenheim [1895–1977], "Studies in the Logic of Explanation," in Hempel, *Aspects of Scientific Explanation* [New York: The Free Press, 1965], 245–295); Hempel, "The Function of General Laws in History," *Aspects*, 231–243.

want them to vote. $C_3$ might be that ecclesiastical authorities refrained from insisting that devout members vote by religion rather than party.

What is to be deduced and thus explained is the further property $F_c$, here simply $F$—the presence of political parties that are cohesive in the national legislature. The minor premise of the argument asserts of a named object or system—in Epstein's case, the Canadian political system—that it meets the conditions specified in the law premise. One then deduces as the conclusion of an argument from both premises a statement asserting that the named object or system, $a$, has the property $F$ as well: "$Fa$," in the symbolism of logic, or "$a$ is $F$." In the present case, the conclusion asserts that the Canadian political system—like everything else covered by the law premise—has cohesive parties, too.

The general form of a covering law explanation, then, is as follows:

(1)  *Premise 1 (the law, representing a causal regularity):*

For all $x$, if $x$ is $C_1$ and $C_2$ and $C_3$, etc., then $x$ is $F$; that is to say, $x$ has the property $F$ also.

(2)  *Premise 2 (the object and its circumstances):*

$a$ is $C_1$ and $C_2$ and $C_3$, etc.

(3)  *Conclusion (the case that was brought up for explanation):*

$a$ is $F$, or $Fa$.

Whether this form is general enough to accommodate all forms of scientific explanation is questionable. Not everything that counts as an explanation is a full-fledged argument. Some philosophers have held that the most general form of explanation consists simply in stating a relevant probability, with the covering law form figuring as a special case in which the probability of the object's being $F$, given that it is $C_1$, $C_2$, and $C_3$, etc., approaches certainty.[3] Are explanations of a statistical form attempted more frequently? In the social sciences, daunted by the odds against finding a law that works with certainty, researchers may be tempted to say yes. They may, however, be failing to distinguish between an exact statistical law, with a precise probability figure of an object's being $F$, and an inexact one, in which $a$'s being $F$ is merely said to be "highly probable" or "more probable than not." An exact statistical law, one might think, would be as hard to come by as a categorical one with certainty. On the other hand, an inexact statistical law may not, in upshot, differ very much from a categorical one in which "etc."—the *ceteris paribus*, or "other things being equal" clause— allows for a good deal of looseness in the fit between the law and observations. It might still be worthwhile to assert a loose categorical law, but only when one is ready to assert that notwithstanding the *ceteris paribus* clause about unspecified conditions, $x$ is $F$ is probable given the specified

[3]Wesley C. Salmon, *Statistical Explanation and Statistical Relevance* (Pittsburgh: University of Pittsburgh Press, 1971).

conditions. Let this probable judgment serve as a proviso for accepting the corresponding loose categorical law.

Frequently aimed at or not, and however loosely realized in practice, the covering law form of explanation offers a useful model for the relation between explanation and prediction. It also offers a useful model for the relation between both of these ideas and testing by experiment or observation. If we begin by knowing that $a$ is $F$, supplying (1) and (2) gives us an explanation of this fact—provided that (1) has a certain character not established simply by its having a universally quantified form, a matter to be discussed in a moment. If we begin by knowing (1) and (2), then we are in a position not just to guess that $a$ will be found to be $F$ but to make a scientifically based prediction that it will be. Finally, we may not know (1) or $Fa$, either, but we may be led to hypothesize (1). Then we try to find or to bring about an $a$ that satisfies (2). If we then observe $Fa$, we have done something to confirm (1). We shall never have done enough to confirm it once and for all, beyond the power of further events to upset it. But such an upset, too, is of scientific interest. If we maintain after observation that $a$ is not $F$ after all, and we continue maintaining (2), (1) has been falsified.

The covering law form also lends ready aid to relating the idea of cause to the idea of scientific explanation. I follow J. L. Mackie (1917–1981) in the outlines of his treatment of the concept of cause and derive from him the notion of "an INUS condition."[4] What is an INUS condition and how do we get to this notion?

The first move to make is to expand the form of the law premise representing the causal regularity at issue. Let the antecedent be generalized to cover a number of different combinations of conditions, each sufficient for $Fx$. On the way to doing that, we may recognize that not only may Epstein have left unmentioned some of the conditions that must combine with the British parliamentary system. He may also have disregarded different combinations of conditions that would also have had the effect of cohesive parties. In one such combination, instead of the British parliamentary system, there might be an arrangement whereby candidates pledged themselves to vote with their parties in the legislature on pain of having to submit to a recall election if they did not.

We may accordingly expand the law premise offered by Epstein to the following:

(1)′ For all $x$, or for all political systems, if either $(C_1)$ $x$ has the British parliamentary system and conditions $C_2$, $C_3$, etc., or $(C_{10})x$ has the pledge-and-recall system and other conditions $C_{11}$, $C_{12}$, etc., then $x$ will have cohesive parties.

Following Mackie, we now say, second, that a cause is "at least an INUS condition," which is to say it has at least the role that an individual condition

[4]J. L. Mackie, *The Cement of the Universe* (Oxford: Clarendon Press, 1974), 62.

$C$ belonging to one of these combinations has in bringing about $Fx$. What is that role—the role, for example, of $C_{11}$, the second-named condition in the second combination? Inspection of the logical character of (1)′ tells us that [given the truth of (1)′] the role is this: Such a condition is an Insufficient but Necessary component in an Unnecessary but Sufficient combination of conditions for bringing about $Fx$ (hence the acronym "INUS"). In our example, there are just two sufficient combinations; in other cases there might be many more than two. In every case, each sufficient combination will furnish us with an assertible law with the same simpler, contracted form of Epstein's finding.

Mackie's analysis clears up the long-standing confusion about whether a cause is a necessary condition or a sufficient condition or neither or both. In the context of (1)′, $C_1$ is by itself neither; but given $C_2$, $C_3$, etc., it is a sufficient condition for $Fx$. If we are asking whether $C_2$, etc., can bring about $Fx$, we can say yes, provided that the necessary condition of $C_1$ is also met. We may also, of course, treat any whole combination taken by itself as the cause of $Fx$; understood in this way, the cause is a sufficient condition. If, by exception, it is the only combination of conditions sufficient to bring about $Fx$, then it is a necessary condition, too.

The generalized formula (1)′ and the notion of "at least an INUS condition" do not suffice to capture the notion of a cause. We must rule out merely definitional connections, like ascribing the cohesiveness of Canadian political parties to their voting as blocs. Contemporary philosophical discussion has established that this will not always be easy to do. It will not always be easy to determine whether a given condition should be regarded as definitional. When, however, it has been decided that a condition should be regarded as definitional, it must be ruled out as a causal condition.

We must also rule out, by some combination of background knowledge with assumption, the possibility that some pair of antecedent and consequent in the formula represents joint effects of the same underlying cause rather than cause and effect, respectively. To cite standard examples, the lower reading on a barometer and the coming of a storm are both effects of lower air pressure, and the coming of day, like the coming of night, is an effect of the earth's rotation in the presence of the sun.

To our account of what a causal condition amounts to we must add something about temporal priority and something about counterfactual conditionals. On temporal priority, I shall say only this: In some applications, we can and do take $Fa$ to have occurred prior to the conditions from which it can be deduced. For example, from the effects of an eruption, we infer that a volcano $a$ erupted earlier. Such applications do not bring into question the capacity of (1)′ to express lawlike connections. We can perfectly well invoke lawlike connections in reverse order of time: Whenever a deposit of lava is present, a volcano erupted earlier to produce it. However, it is at least controversial whether we can have causes occurring after their effects. Georg H. von Wright, whose definition of cause will be repeatedly cited in this book, defines a cause in terms of what we can do to produce or prevent something's happening.[5] This implies what many suppose to be a firmly seated feature of our ordinary use of the term "cause." On that supposition, the term applies to forward-running—or to simultaneous—connections only. I shall go along with Mackie, von Wright, and this supposition about ordinary language. For (1)' to express a causal law, I shall hold, the conditions must be temporally prior to $Fx$ or at least concurrent with it.

The point about counterfactuals takes us into deeper water, where no adequate analysis is yet available.[6] This much seems clear: When we assert something in the form of (1)' as a causal law, we are ready to assert, on the basis of the same evidence, a number of counterfactuals. We are ready to assert, for example, that in cases where none of those combinations of conditions did obtain, $Fx$ would nevertheless have been brought about if one of them (one of the combinations) had; that given $C_{11}$, $C_{41}$, etc., in such a case, $Fx$ would have resulted if only $C_{32}$ had held as well; that if $Fx$ had failed to come about in the present case, then none of the combinations would have obtained; and so forth.

## FALSIFIABILITY

It is an embarrassment that we are not able to say just what it is about the evidence that leads us to assert both (1)' and the associated counterfactuals. Perhaps most of this embarrassment is due to the grip of a conception of knowledge that induces us to demand evidence fully justifying us in our assertions. If "fully justifying" means "ruling out any possibility of being mistaken," none of our empirical findings about the world have such evidence. So none of them is genuine knowledge if knowledge requires such evidence. Here Popper's insistence upon falsifiability is helpful.[7] The universal generalizations that we claim to know about the world must all be falsifiable, if they are to be about the world in the sense of making empirical assertions. Otherwise, we can go on maintaining them no matter what we observe, and the connection with observation, which we seek in empirical inquiry, is broken. But if causal laws are falsifiable, they must remain open to doubt in principle after any finite number of observations and even after any finite number of rigorous attempts to falsify them. They can have for us no more than the status of hypotheses that have survived all the tests which they have been put to so far.

The test of falsifiability has to be handled with some care if it is to

[5]Georg H. von Wright, *Explanation and Understanding* (Ithaca, N.Y.: Cornell University Press, 1971), 70.

[6]For a survey of the disputes about counterfactuals (and other conditional statements), see J. L. Mackie, *Truth, Probability, and Paradox* (Oxford: Clarendon Press, 1973), 64–119.

[7]Popper, *Logic of Discovery*, 40–42.

accord with its use in science. When we are using the covering law model in testing a hypothesis, we are not bound to count the hypothesis falsified if $a$ turns out not to be $F$. We always have the alternative of rejecting the minor premise. The historian of science Thomas Kuhn has maintained against Popper that scientists in fact frequently do this.[8] In the practice of what Kuhn calls "normal science," they accept the truth of hypotheses that belong to the paradigm or to its past applications and write off negative findings as due to lapses of experimental method. Even if the hypothesis at issue is held to have been falsified, moreover, we have, as Kuhn and other commentators would insist, some discretion about how to bring this fact to bear upon any wider theory to which the hypothesis belonged. Instead of taking the negative finding to falsify the whole theory, we may take it to have falsified, through falsifying the present hypothesis, some part of the theory or other, with a choice left to us which part. Ultimately, however, empirical hypotheses and theories must stand or fall with observation. They will be counted as falsified when the negative findings become too prominent and alternative theories free of the anomalies are available.

## LOOSE REGULARITIES

If the law premise is loose and concedes its looseness in a *ceteris paribus* clause, there is little danger of its being rejected out of hand with one contrary observation. But then does it give enough of an opening to the test of falsifiability to rank as an empirical law of any sort? Is not the regularity that it represents all too typical of the regularities of social phenomena in being riddled with exceptions? The regularities that social science discovers may seem, typically, too loose to be expressed as causal laws. They may also seem too superficial, since just knowing that one phenomenon regularly (though perhaps only with loose regularity) follows another seems always to beg the question why.

The chief point that I want to make about looseness is that however low we set the standard for being a causal law we run the risk of discarding useful information. Philosophers who demand a very high standard of reliability for causal generalizations may be unwilling to grant that social science has any causal laws to offer at all. But then what is to be done about the imperfect approximations that social science can offer about the effects of the British parliamentary system, for example, or about the forms that despair takes with the men on Tally's Corner? These approximations are all too likely to lose all philosophical credit and fall into neglect, at least by philosophers. Accepting them as causal regularities keeps them in view

[8]See the contributions by Kuhn and Popper to Imre Lakatos and Alan Musgrave, eds., *Criticism and the Growth of Knowledge* (Cambridge: Cambridge University Press, 1970).

and allows them to serve pending refinement. I am inclined to think that a standard relaxed enough to recognize causal regularities that hold substantially more often than not—say, at least two-thirds of the time—is appropriate. Thus we can allow for probabilistic statements or tendency statements—when these approximate universal lawlike statements. By covering the exceptions under "other things being equal," furthermore, we can retain direct use of the covering law form as the simplest model of explanation.

Counting against this relaxed standard for regularities, of course, is the jeopardy in which acceptance of loose causal generalizations puts having any trenchant standard of confirmation or falsification. Does it not fly in the face of Popper's impressive insistence that hypotheses must be falsifiable or else anything goes? A loose causal generalization can be saved from falsification in any particular instance by invoking the *ceteris paribus* clause. I am not, however, suggesting that anything goes. Most instances must not be deviant. The test of falsifiability still applies, though not by directly confronting the lawlike premise with any single contrary instance. It applies in comparing the proportion of contrary instances with the probable judgment that was a proviso for accepting the law notwithstanding the *ceteris paribus* clause. According to that probable judgment, the effect must happen substantially more often than not.

## SUPERFICIAL CONNECTIONS

The risk of discarding useful information is also the chief point to be made about superficiality. Some philosophers will be unhappy that regularities which I would reckon as genuine may acquire that status without anyone's making sure that they mention, or even imply, "causal powers" among the conditions or some sort of causal mechanism connecting the conditions with the effects. If so, we may have a law—such a connection—in hand and not really understand how it operates. Most people are in this position with respect to the causal connection between turning the key to start an automobile engine and the engine's starting. Epstein (and his readers) would have been in this position had he stopped with his finding of a regularity connecting the British parliamentary system and party discipline. (As we shall see, he does descend to a lower level of facts to explain how the individual Members of Parliament acted to give cohesive results.)

I am not arguing that social science, in its accounts of causation, should stop with superficial connections when there are underlying mechanisms or powers to be brought to light. What I wish to say is that superficial though they may often be, as well as loose, the connections in question deserve some respect. They are facts, even if they are superficial facts. It is better to be informed about them superficially than not be informed at all. Of course, the information should be propagated only with warnings about its limits and about the dangers of being misled when such dangers arise—for instance, from ideological tendencies to omit unsettling qualifications. The basic principle, that it is better to be informed than not, stands nevertheless. On that principle, again, the causal inquiries of social science can be decisively justified, even if their results almost always leave much to be desired that can often be had in natural science.

## TRANSITORY LAWS

A more important drawback to the causal laws discovered by social science than looseness and superficiality is their liability to stop being laws. The regularities that they represent may disappear when one's view shifts, in time or space, from a given society and culture to another. There is an ever-present possibility that people even in one given society will do unanticipated and inexplicable things. This possibility, because it is realized less often, may threaten the stability of social regularities less than the equally ever-present possibility that people will choose, on grounds explicable at least person by person, to live and act differently. But the two possibilities work together in demanding concessions apparently incompatible with giving laws in social science the firm, inexorable foundation that many would expect causal laws to have.

Now, we could keep up a claim to universality by rewriting any lapsed laws to specify that they applied only under circumstances in all relevant respects like those at the time of the society and culture for which they were asserted. However, that move is a bit of a cheat—in it we use "all relevant respects" to evade further empirical testing. Moreover, paradoxical as it may be to treat any causal laws as transitory (and limited in geographical or demographical scope), social science has nothing to fear from such treatment. It has in fact something to gain, since such treatment puts an honest face on a difference between social science and natural science that would otherwise be a festering source of embarrassment.

Treating causal laws as genuine even if transitory has an eminent precedent in social science. Marx did not deny that there were laws of the market. He did not deny either that his forerunners—the other economists of the British classical school in particular, from Adam Smith (1723–1790) to David Ricardo (1772–1823) and later—had given an appropriate account of these laws, so far as their account went. He himself treated the laws that they had discovered, and the laws that he added to them, as inexorable causal laws. Given industries equally capital intensive, exchange value could not, while the market operates, deviate long from a quantity proportional to labor input. Again, the wages of labor will, in the presence of an Industrial Reserve Army, inevitably be reduced, and with them the living standard of the masses, to the subsistence level. What Marx contended was that these laws held only while capitalism persisted.[9] The failing of other economists was thinking that the laws were permanent, overlooking the features of capitalism that were already making its survival precarious and would in the end lead to its destruction.

Moreover, the condition of being possibly transitory is something that may reasonably be attached even to the causal laws of natural science. Would it substantially discredit natural science if the laws of one epoch—the laws prevailing since the most recent big bang—were different from the laws of another, say, the previous period of contraction? True, it is an important consolation if the epoch lasts millions of years rather than for the time of one human generation or less. Nevertheless, the logical allowance for the possibility is the same in principle. It would still be worth knowing what current laws are even if they last only for (say) twenty years. A lot of living and a lot of social policy can be crammed into twenty years. And may not most of the succeeding laws be close cousins of those now current?

The possibility of being limited geographically and demographically calls for a similar allowance. The laws of one region are even now all that some branches of natural science have to offer. Biology has studied only life on earth. Geology, too, has studied only terrestrial phenomena. We may find parallel phenomena elsewhere. Whether we do or not, however, the findings, including the causal regularities, that pertain to the earth deserve scientific respect. The position in social science, when we shift beyond one culture and ask how our findings apply to another, is the same.

## MODEL-THEORETIC VIEW OF SCIENCE

What I have been saying about individual causal laws could be translated into fashionable model-theoretic terms.[10] Let us suppose that we take a number of causal generalizations (loose or exact) and incorporate them simultaneously into the definition of a type of institution or society. Then to be assigned to an institution or a society of that type, real social phenomena must conform to those laws. Phenomena that do conform furnish a model to which the definition applies. It suffices to find one such model,

[9]For example, Karl Marx, *Capital*, trans. Ben Fowkes (London: Penguin, 1976), Preface to the First [German] Edition [1867], 90–91, and pt. 1, chap. 1, sec. 4, "The Fetishism of the Commodity and Its Secret," 163–177.

[10]Here, as I was in the remarks about biology and geology in the previous paragraph, I am following chiefly Ronald Giere's account in an unpublished paper. For a brief standard account of the model-theoretic approach, see Bas C. van Fraassen, *The Scientific Image* (Oxford: Clarendon Press, 1980), 41–69.

unique in space and time, to make the definition an empirically useful and empirically vindicated theory. Indeed, we may be content, so far as use and vindication go, to have a definition that fits a simplified analogue of a real institution or society. The analogue will be a model, both in the sense of being something that answers to the definition or theory and in the sense of being something that on selected points of interest resembles the institution or society.

Can we say that the difference between social science and some branches of natural science (for example, the physics of macroscopic objects within the solar system) is that the former is more often called upon than the latter to deal with changes in phenomena as it shifts from considering phenomena in one region of space and time to another? That is to say, it must revise its theories more often to fit an external reality the nature of which is ascertained somehow (it is a problem how) independently of any theory being tested for fit. It is consequently more often called upon by changes in phenomena to change its definitions and analogues.

Many philosophers have been troubled by the problem about describing reality independently of the very theories that are to be compared with it. What is to go into the description if these theories do not? Some philosophers have turned to a position called "internal realism," which is consistent with definitions and analogues changing more frequently in social science but seems to make this an arbitrary and insignificant difference. Internal realism holds that reality is entirely defined by our theories.[11] We may have definitions or theories changing with different frequency in the natural and social sciences, but the reasons for change are entirely internal. Nothing in the phenomena can compel changes in a theory (a point that may provoke some resistance from residual empiricists). We change theories (definitions, analogues) as we invent new paradigms; and with each change what we regard as reality changes. But we may refuse to change; and, given internal realism, we can supposedly do so without creating insuperable difficulties for ourselves.

Given either internal realism or external realism, the scientific status of our work remains after renouncing claims of universal application for it. We could still, of course, be using universally quantified statements in setting forth the defined predicate that serves as our model or theory. If these statements were exact—at the limit omitting any *ceteris paribus* clauses—they would almost inevitably apply only to a simplified analogue rather than to a real society. The looseness of our empirical knowledge would then be transposed from inside our lawlike statements to the gap between our model and the society described in detail.

[11]The notion of internal realism is due to Hilary Putnam. See, for example, his *Reason, Truth and History* (Cambridge: Cambridge University Press, 1981), 49–74, 119–124.

## GROUP FACTS VERSUS PERSON FACTS

Epstein's finding expresses a causal connection between the presence of one social institution (the British parliamentary system) and the performance of other institutions (political parties in the legislature). The institutions on either side of the connection would not exist, or have the properties that they exhibit, if there were not a number of human beings taking part in them and doing things that in the end justify ascribing the properties to the institutions. Is there anything more to the institutions and their properties than what the people who belong to them do? The property of being cohesive in the legislature comes perhaps as close to being nothing more as any property of social institutions gets. For saying that Canadian political parties are cohesive in this way may well seem to amount just to saying that $M_1$, $M_2$, $M_3$, and others, the Members of Parliament belonging to one party, each vote the way the others do, while $M_{67}$, $M_{68}$, $M_{69}$, and others, Members of Parliament belonging to another party (any other party), each vote in the way the others in that party do.

Now, clearly the cohesiveness of the parties does imply that Members of Parliament vote in the ways described. Yet cohesiveness is not a fact interchangeable with anything that individual Members of Parliament do one by one. It is a fact, in each case in which it is a fact, about a group—a party in Parliament—not a fact about any of the individual people who belong to the party. No individual Member of Parliament votes all in the same way—as a cohesive bloc—just as no individual Member of Parliament has a majority in Parliament. At the very least the person facts about individual Members have to be put together before we have a group fact.

Is a group fact anything more than person facts put together in a conjunction? Even cohesiveness is more than this. It is certainly more than a conjunction of person facts none of which need mention the groups about which cohesiveness is a fact. To say that the Canadian parties are cohesive is not to say only that the Members of Parliament who belong to them at present vote as blocs. It is to say that whatever people might replace them as being at once members of the parties and Members of Parliament would vote as blocs. Most of these people, even if we include among them only present Canadian citizens eligible for election to Parliament, have never cast a vote in Parliament; most of them never will. They are connected with the group fact of cohesiveness only through the possibility of belonging to parties in Parliament; and to describe this possibility the parties (as well as Parliament) must be mentioned under some description.

Furthermore, belonging—or having the possibility of belonging—to the groups in question is not something that can be determined solely by considering persons one by one and their physical settings. The groups and their principles of constitution must be considered in order to identify the persons who are members already or who have just become such. The principles may be quite complex and may embrace a number of stringent rules about eligibility, nomination, and election. Similar complications may be expected with other person facts related to cohesiveness, including the central person facts of voting one way or another. It is hard to see how the principles on which parties in Parliament are constituted could fail to have implications about what is to count as voting. In any case, there must be rules that do say what is to count and that can be ascribed to these groups. Whether they are principles of constitution or not, these rules are, like the principles of constitution, facts about the groups.

The parties in Parliament share the rules about what is to count as voting with Parliament itself, which is a group even more complexly institutionalized than the parties. Parliament is a group organized in elaborate ways to act as a group. Members of Parliament take on specific roles as Speaker, presiding over debates; Ministers, bringing in projects of legislation; Leader of the Opposition, challenging the merits of the projects. The bills are normally enacted after a number of rounds of discussion because a majority of Members, consisting of Members belonging to the party in power (to which all the Members who are Ministers belong, too), vote to enact it. This elaborate system of rules and roles cannot be described solely by a conjunction of simple person facts in which nothing describing the system is implied.

Not all groups are so highly institutionalized; not all groups are so highly institutionalized as political parties (or the subsets of members of political parties who are Members of Parliament). The distinction between group facts and conjunctions of person facts will fade if we consider successively less institutionalized groups. Finally, when we are dealing with a mob, or with a collection of people who happen to be found together for a moment in a bus, the distinction may fade out altogether. But then we are dealing with collections of people that social scientists will resist calling "groups."

Highly institutionalized or not, groups may disappear in a way, namely by being disbanded, that leaves the individual persons who belonged to them continuing. There is no way, however, in which all the persons, present and future, who belong to a group can disappear without the group disappearing, too. This point does not, however, impair the reality of group facts or make them less consequential than person facts. On the contrary: In many, perhaps most, cases, group facts are very consequential indeed. They affect other group facts, and they induce individual people to act one way rather than another. Think, for example, of the group fact that consists in one party's winning a majority of seats in Parliament.

Philosophers have concerned themselves with these points about group facts and person facts in the course of discussing a famous doctrine known as "methodological individualism." The final fallback position for this doctrine may be the controversial thesis that the only ultimately satisfactory strategy of explanation in the social sciences is one that moves from person facts to explain group facts and not the other way around.[12] My remarks about group facts and person facts leave this position untouched. I have not said anything about strategies of explanation. On the other hand, my remarks also leave open the possibility that some strategies will indeed move the other way, or move from group facts to group facts, and, along with the strategy (which is not at issue) that would explain person facts by person facts, all be equally valid and satisfactory.

## NATURALISTIC PERSON FACTS

Are the person facts in Epstein's study—the facts about individual Members of Parliament—interpretative facts or naturalistic ones? I shall in due time be making the point that there are interpretative person facts in Epstein's study, playing an important part at the micro level in the explanation that he offers of the cohesiveness of Canadian parties in Parliament. At this juncture, it is more important to make the point that there are, characteristically, person facts as well as group facts on the naturalistic side of social science. Epstein's study was brought forward in the first instance to illustrate the naturalistic side with group facts characteristic of it. Such facts are characteristically overlooked by champions of the interpretative view, who tend to think of social science as occupied entirely with the actions of individual persons who have others in mind. One should not be misled. There are also naturalistic person facts, and some of them can be found in Epstein.

At first sight, it is true, the crucial person facts there look like interpretative facts because they apparently belong to the theory of rational choice. Individual Members of Parliament vote with their parties out of self-interest. If they are members of the governing party, they do not want the government to fall, which will send them out to campaign for the renewed endorsement by their constituencies. If they are members of an opposition party, they do not want to give the public the impression that the party is too undisciplined to carry on the government.

Some naturalistic person facts come to light, however, when the theory of rational choice is transformed into a naturalistic theory. One way of doing this is to construct preference maps for individual decision makers

[12]Popper endorses methodological individualism in *Poverty of Historicism,* 136. The fallback position emerges in the course of Arthur C. Danto's dissection of the issues arising about the doctrine, in *Analytical Philosophy of History* (Cambridge: Cambridge University Press, 1965), 257–284. See also David Copp, "What Collectives Are: Agency, Individualism and Legal Theory," *Dialogue* 23 (1984): 249–269.

from observing what they actually choose as their resources (e.g., their money incomes) and the prices of the goods offered them vary. Then one may hypothesize that the maps will hold during subsequent choice situations. If the predictions implied are actually confirmed one has in hand a naturalistic theory of the decision makers' behavior. No testimony from them is called for, nor any evidence about their further purposes and larger views. Specific incomes and specific prices will have, given the dispositions registered in the preference maps, the causal effect of having a certain combination of goods taken rather than any other.

Another route to person facts fitting into a naturalistic perspective lies through psychological behaviorism. This approach aims to find conditions that reinforce patterns of behavior exhibited by the person being studied. It leads as well to observing the speed with which various schedules of reinforcement lead to the pattern's becoming a persistent one when the preceding circumstances are repeated. One may also measure how long the pattern persists through a succession of such circumstances when the reinforcing condition is not fulfilled. Clearly counting, measuring, and comparing numbers with the aim of establishing relationships between quantitative variables are all involved in such inquiries. Moreover, the relationships are causal ones. The cause of the pattern's becoming a persistent one is the repetition of reinforcers on a suitable schedule. A suitably intermittent schedule of reinforcement is a more effective cause than a regular one. Stimuli associated with reinforcement in the past will elicit—will cause to be forthcoming—an instance of the pattern now.

If the patterns induced by schedules of reinforcement were all trivial ones (such as picking up one's fork before one's knife, or tending to move to the right of a person encountered rather than to the left), they would still be within the province of social phenomena—of human phenomena in a social setting and subject to human choices. This would be true, too, even if the reinforcers were physical and such that they could have operated outside a social setting. In fact, the patterns may be quite important ones, and the reinforcers themselves may be social phenomena. Such is the case when the reinforcers are actions conferring rewards or imposing punishments. They still fall within causal schemes, and those schemes are examples of naturalistic social science.

Naturalistic person facts can be found in Epstein's study on both approaches. The preference maps of the Members of Parliament are such as to give, persistently, priority to voting with their parties over any attraction that might lie in voting otherwise. The attraction rejected might be the applause, perhaps with material support, of various public-spirited groups or the support of special interests in their constituencies. But it is no accident that the members' preference maps take this form. As party members, they have been brought within a scheme of reinforcements, positive and negative, that shape their maps and their behavior to conform with party discipline. Long before a Member of Parliament even contemplates voting at odds with her party—before she even wins her seat—she will have been reinforced when she upheld party policies and checked when she showed any signs of getting out of line.

## USES AND ABUSES OF QUANTITIES

Though Epstein's chief thesis—that it is the presence of the British parliamentary system that causes Canadian parties to be cohesive in Parliament—is not quantitative, it has quantitative implications. One such implication lies in the general causal law implied: The law, as it approaches perfect formulation, holds only if every time the cause (the British parliamentary system taken together with other conditions) is present, the effect (disciplined parliamentary parties) is present, too. That is a very stringent statistical requirement. Other quantitative implications demand evidence of cohesive voting on any one occasion—the count must show that all members of a given party vote one way if they vote at all—and evidence of cohesive voting repeated on one occasion after another.

Such quantitative themes are typical of naturalistic social science. They are elsewhere explicitly developed to a degree that Epstein does not attempt. The development, to advocates of the interpretative view, offers a good deal of provocation. The philosophers who champion the interpretative side of social science typically not only fail to see that there is (except in the way of a misguided pretense) a naturalistic side at all, or at least fail to concede it much substance. They are typically innumerate—indeed, antinumerate—to a degree that would have shocked Plato, for whom the ascent to wisdom lay through the study of mathematics. They dislike and distrust quantitative methods, looking upon them as characteristic of naturalistic methods. So they are inclined to scorn quantitative methods and denounce them as inappropriate to the study of social phenomena.

I think this inclination is wrongheaded, but I would concede that the inclination is not entirely baseless prejudice. It originates in part in apprehensions, not themselves unreasonable, about excessive simplification, excessive abstraction, even (with spurious quantities) actual confusion. With or without these abuses, formal methods may tend to impair, in those who employ them without reservations, intuitive powers of interpreting social phenomena. I respect those powers. I agree that a lot of knowledge is yet to be gained with them by people who may themselves have no occasion to make more than the most primitive use of formal methods. I have no intention whatever of bringing forward what the French mathematician and philosopher Pascal (1623–1662), during the ascent of natural science in the seventeenth century, called "the geometrical mind" to supplant fine minds more capable of subtly balancing particulars.[13]

Moreover, the concession that quantities are sometimes used in suspect ways must be honored. An essentially simple but telling example can be found in some flights of desision theory, where there is a tendency for social scientists to elaborate a priori examples in which the quantities of costs and benefits along with numerical probabilities are all supposed to be present. Such theorists forget that many of those quantities will turn up missing in real-life choice situations. They delude themselves and others into thinking that the prescriptions of the theory can be carried out or approximated when more often than not they cannot be. Even more perniciously—in a way that has been noticed and denounced by philosophers opposed anyhow to the use of quantitative methods—the prescriptions are often carried out for just those costs and benefits for which the quantities are known, as if other costs and benefits could be ignored. In such cases, the theory is likely both to give bad advice when taken normatively and, when taken descriptively, to misjudge what people will actually do. For the people who actually have to make the choices may be aware of the considerations that have not been expressed quantitatively and give those considerations decisive weight. If they are not aware, or if they allow the misgivings they may feel to be overridden, they may be horribly disappointed.

On the other hand, quantities—especially quantities suited to statistical treatment—are ubiquitous in social phenomena. We are continually called upon to consider not the mass or velocity of a single body but a number of persons together and such group facts as their mean or median incomes and the mean or median number of days on which they were employed last year. But there are statistics to look for even in the study of an individual person: In what proportion of the votes taken in the session just past did he vote with his party? The naturalistic side of social science quite properly seizes upon statistical quantities in inquiries looking for more precise specifications of causes, more precise causal laws, more exact causal theories. It is continually comparing the variation in one statistic with the variation in another.

## QUANTITATIVE METHODS ILLUSTRATED

In certain applications of quantitative methods to the themes already illustrated, the conception of the facts is deepened by more exact naturalistic, quantitative treatment. Social scientists might, for example, want to study

[13]Blaise Pascal, *Pensées*, in *L'Oeuvre de Pascal*, ed. Jacques Chevalier (Paris: Gallimard, 1950), 826.

the cohesiveness of parties in Parliament more closely than Epstein did. For that purpose they might construct a precise measure for cohesiveness. That is what Samuel Beer did when he undertook to discover just how the cohesiveness of the parties in the British Parliament had varied over the period from 1860 to 1946. Beer's "index of cohesion" for a given party equals "the difference between the percentages of party members voting on each side. . . . If 60% vote one way and 40% the other then the value of the index is 60 − 40 = 20. When cohesion is complete the value of the index is 100 − 0 = 100, and at the other extreme the index is 50 − 50 = 0."[14] Averaged over each year's voting, the index for each of the two major parties rose from about 60 in 1860 to 99 in 1945–46.

With this finding, the measure has already given an answer to a question characteristic of the naturalistic approach to social science. For on the naturalistic side, social scientists are always asking precisely how does a feature of the phenomena vary over time and wanting a quantitative answer. But Beer's index also opens the way to further naturalistic questions. How does the exhibited variation in cohesiveness relate to variation in other matters, which one might hypothesize are related? It would be interesting to have in this connection, though hard to get, a measure of the power concentrated in the Prime Minister. One might expect that to vary in the same direction as Beer's index. Or one might look for a measure of the increase in the business that Parliament had to deal with. In more leisurely days, before the rise of the welfare state and other heavy burdens in economic policy for the state, was discipline less needed to get through legislative business with minimal efficiency? This question points to a possible cause for the increase in cohesiveness. But so does the question about the Prime Minister's power, though there one might wonder whether the causal connection did not run in the other direction, to the increase in the Prime Minister's power from the increase in cohesion.

Further examples of the naturalistic use of quantitative methods can be found in the treatment that social scientists have accorded some of the themes present in Liebow's book. Quantitative methods and the naturalistic approach are equally appropriate here. I present two examples. One has to do with unemployment and the other with friendship, both matters of special concern to Liebow.

A diagram (Figure 1), taken from the article by Martin Bronfenbrenner on inflation and deflation in *The International Encyclopedia of Social Sciences*, comes with the first example.[15]

---

[14]Samuel Beer, *Modern British Politics* (London: Faber, 1965), 257ff.; cited and explained in David J. Bartholomew and Edward E. Bassett, *Let's Look at the Figures: The Quantitative Approach to Human Affairs* (London: Penguin, 1971), 20–21.

[15]Figure from "Inflation and Deflation" by Martin Bronfenbrenner. Reprinted by permission of the publisher from *International Encyclopedia of Social Sciences*, David L. Sills, Editor. Vol. 7, page 293. Copyright © 1968 by Crowell Collier and Macmillan, Inc.

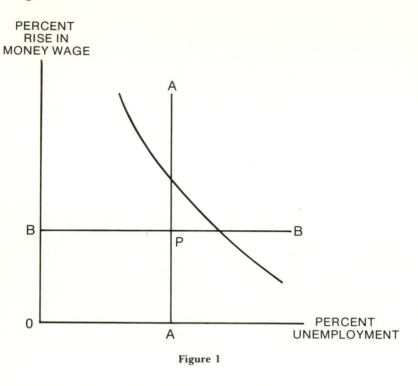

**Figure 1**

At point *P* line *A*, showing the percentage of unemployment accepted as the maximum politically tolerable, meets line *B*, showing the percentage rise in money wages accepted as tolerable. The curve that lies beyond *P* is the famous Phillips Curve, so named for the economist A. W. Phillips (1914–1975). As shown in the diagram, it expresses the hypothesis that one cannot reduce the amount of unemployment to the tolerable level without creating an intolerable amount of inflation.

What is tolerable, either in the way of unemployment or in the way of inflation, is, one may suppose, dependent on people's opinions, which may be variable, indeed, volatile. So the relative positions of *P* and of the Phillips Curve may not be firmly founded. Furthermore, any such curve may greatly exaggerate the precision with which rises in employment are related to rises in money wage rates. The more exact the relation is, the more one would suspect that it is transient: All sorts of processes—technological change, unionization, changes in the organization of work, changes in location—must be going on that would affect the quantities. The very notion of unemployment is to a degree arbitrary: If you decide not to count as unemployed people who have given up looking for work, what are you going to count as giving up? The notion of money wages, as a statistic, is not in much better shape.

On all these grounds, one may regard the Phillips Curve as a rather soft fact, even if (something that has been vigorously disputed) it does currently hold, at least roughly, given reasonable definitions of money wages and unemployment. (Phillips himself argued that the curve relationship has held in the United Kingdom since the 1860s.)[16] I am concerned not to defend its being a fact, but solely to make the point that if it is a fact, it is a suitable sort of fact for social science to notice. Certainly it is important: It would explain, in part, why there were not enough decent jobs available for the men on Tally's Corner. It would also explain why there was not much prospect of remedy within the political and economic systems as they stand. Anyone who wanted to make more jobs available would be steered by this finding to asking what in the underlying arrangements of the society could be changed so that a remedy became feasible.

The finding itself, however soft, however important, is a naturalistic one. To begin with, the Phillips Curve itself is a naturalistic fact about how variation in one quantity is related to variation in another. Carry your eye along the horizontal axis and halt at some figure for percent unemployed; then the point directly above, on the curve, gives the percent increase in money wages that may, on the evidence, be expected to consort with that amount of unemployment. The curve is not a rule, which the members of the society have adopted or come to accept, and which they could repeal by legislation at any moment. No agent or collection of agents is called upon to do anything to fulfill it. It does not lay down conditions that are to be met by anyone who wishes to perform an action that will be categorized and understood in some particular way. Rather, it says that whether change in the one variable is the effect of deliberate policy or just something that unwittingly has been allowed to happen, the other variable will change in a certain way. Moreover, however volatile people's opinions are on the normative questions about what amounts of unemployment and inflation are tolerable, if point $P$ represents a consensus answer to both questions, then the relationship of that point to points on the Phillips Curve is a naturalistic group fact about the society under study.

My second illustration of quantitative methods applied to the subject matter of Liebow's book is one that has been singled out for scornful attack by opponents of naturalistic social science. The sociologist George

---

[16]A. W. Phillips, "The Relation Between Unemployment and the Rate of Change of Money Wage Rates in the United Kingdom: 1861–1957," *Economica*, New Series, 25 (1958): 283–299. For current sophisticated use of the notion of the Phillips Curve see, for example, John Cornwall, *The Conditions for Economic Recovery* (Oxford: Martin Robertson, 1983), 26–28, 45–50.

Homans, in a study of a variety of social groups, arrived at the following generalization about friendship:

If the interactions between the members of a group are frequent in the external system, sentiments of liking will grow up between them, and these sentiments will in turn lead to further interactions, over and above the interactions of the external system.[17]

Herbert A. Simon, a social scientist of multiple interests, among them the advancement of quantitative methods, seized upon Homans's work and undertook to represent it by a mathematical model containing three related equations, of which the third runs:

$$dW/dt = c_1(I - \gamma W) + c_2(F - W)$$

where $W$ is the (mean) total amount of activity carried on in the group by an average member, $I$ is the level of friendliness (or, Simon says, of "group identification").[18] $c_1$, $c_2$, and $\gamma$ are constants—specific numbers— that determine exactly what values the function will give for changes of $W$ over time. (For the moment, $F$ can be ignored.) When $I = \gamma W$, the level of friendliness and the amount of activity are in equilibrium, implying no tendency in this regard for the activity in the group to increase.

One might wonder just how these quantities are to be measured. What activities make up any person's "total amount of activity" ($W$), and how are they counted? Is the variable $I$ measured by the number of friends that a person reports or the number of times people greet each other in a friendly way? Or (as Simon's alternative term for the variable, "group identification," might suggest) is it measured by scores on a questionnaire about feelings of loyalty and willingness to make sacrifices in a common cause? It is the responsibility of Homans and Simon or of people following their lead to supply such criteria, show that they are matters susceptible of systematic observation, and defend them as capturing at least in part what the terms used to describe them imply.

Whatever criteria are settled upon, it should be clear to a careful reader that the equation does not amount simply to saying that whenever people interact more frequently, they become friendlier. Reading it this way misled one philosophical commentator into the jibe that this was something "no one but a professional social scientist would even have been tempted to believe."[19] The variable for interaction in fact appears not in the present

[17]George C. Homans, *The Human Group* (New York: Harcourt Brace, 1950), 112.

[18]Herbert A. Simon, "Mathematical Constructions in Social Science" (revised version), in *Philosophical Problems of the Social Sciences*, ed. David Braybrooke (New York: Macmillan, 1965), 83–98.

[19]Alasdair MacIntyre, "Causality and History," in *Essays on Explanation and Understanding*, ed. Juha Manninen and Raimo Tuomela (Dordrecht, Holland: Reidel, 1976), 137–158.

equation but in Simon's other two; all three have to be taken into account to obtain Simon's full translation of Homans's generalization. Moreover, $I$, the variable for friendliness, is an aggregative variable, summing up the net results of a variety of facts at the individual level. As such, it may rise with the overall amount of interaction, as Simon's other equations imply, consistently with some pairs of people becoming less friendly with more interaction. Homans's "sentiments of liking," in the aggregate, would behave in the same way.

Furthermore, both Simon's equation and Homans's generalization refer to "the external system," or environment. $F$ in Simon's equation is the amount of activity required by the environment. Simon's equation says that (mean) total activity increases as a function jointly of on the one hand the difference between the level of friendliness and the equilibrium level and on the other hand the difference between the amount of activity required by the external system and the existing amount. If friendliness increases by and large, the amount of effort that members of the group will put into its activity will increase. Homans's generalization specifically restricts the interactions that generate the increased friendliness to interactions in the external system, by which he means that they are interactions occurring in the course of responding to a challenge to a group's survival. In other words, friendliness in the aggregate will increase among people interacting during common tasks imposed on a group by its environment.

Not only is the hypothesis, once understood, not a silly one. It is something that helps solve problems. Why has community life in Framingham, Massachusetts, one of Homans's subjects, disintegrated to an appreciable degree since the town became little more than a suburb of Boston? Homans's hypothesis implies the solution: because the inhabitants no longer form a group cooperating in common tasks that are vital to them. This solution can be used further afield. Why are friendships so loose and fitful for the men on Tally's Corner? Homans's hypothesis suggests that were the men working together to meet their needs, their friendships would be firmer. In fact the men are little more than a pool of casual labor.

## FORMAL METHODS WITHOUT QUANTITIES

Not all formal methods are quantitative. An important example of formal methods applicable with or without quantities lies in the use of logic to construct axiomatized theories. Such theories appear in logic itself. They also, however, include theories with empirical import.

In a system of logic cast in axiomatic form, all the propositions, both axioms and the theorems deduced from them, are truths of logic which hold regardless of observation. In the propositional calculus, they are tautologies: "If $p$, then $p$"; "If it's raining, then it's raining." They thus have nothing to say about whether the world is in one observable state rather than another. In an axiomatized empirical theory, on the other hand, all the propositions, including the axioms, will have empirical content. Whether they are maintained or not will depend on whether they are corroborated by observation. They need not be put to the test of observation one by one. The whole theory, including the axioms, is tested by every observation. With or without quantities, axiomatization can enjoy the advantages of formal methods. These lie in part in the efficiency that they make possible. With abbreviated symbols and with explicit means of transformation one can easily move repeatedly back and forth between thoughts entertained or asserted. The advantages lie in part in the precision that they encourage and at the same time facilitate: precision of terms and properties; precision of comparisons (of the magnitude of the same property in different objects; of the variability of different properties); precision of orientation. The last-named dimension of precision has to do with keeping track of the relations of one thought to another—or to many others—hence of establishing a perspective or orientation. Mentioning it opens the way to mentioning a number of other advantages. These can be collected under the head of the organizing contribution that formal methods make. They are means of imparting structure to thinking and of imputing structure to the world, not just the bits of structure that consist of single regularities and relations, but networks—relations of relations—that bind single regularities to other ones.

It is at this point that projects of axiomatization are invited. Axiomatization can cast structures into forms that are at once specially rigorous (grounding theorems upon axioms) and specially perspicuous (dividing fundamental axioms from theorems, but also in manifesting local relations between theorems). It also supplies a guide to empirical research. On the one hand, an axiomatized theory enables those who possess it to assess the impact of incoming observations, as relevant or irrelevant to the theory and, if relevant, as falling in with the theory or disconfirming it at least in part. The assessment and the guidance of the axiomatized theory do not stop there, since disconfirmation may be dealt with in various ways. The axiomatized theory shows what options exist in the way of theorems and axioms to be given up and how far the disconfirmation in any case reaches through the theory. On the other hand, with an axiomatized theory in hand, those who possess it can specify gaps in empirical evidence and possible extensions—new theorems to be added, with or without new axioms—and hence specify opportunities for useful research.

In the branches of social science that have accumulated a wealth of observations without much elaborate theory, social scientists have been prone to miss the point of attempts at axiomatization. Inevitably, at the outset, such attempts will if they are serious make use of observations and generalizations already familiar to the social scientists in the field, who may react by thinking that they are being told only what they already know. An axiomatization of the theory of party competition, or of Epstein's account of political parties within or without the British parliamentary system, might have this effect. So would an axiomatization of Liebow's study. Even in such beginnings with familiar ideas, however, axiomatization may logically require the resolution of certain outstanding issues and show that they can be resolved consistently with the evidence one way rather than another. Thus axiomatization of the theory of party competition can show precisely how bipolarization of party competition in single-member constituencies may fail to lead to bipolarization in all constituencies taken together.[20]

## A SCALE OF SCIENTIFICITY

Axiomatization, when it is intelligently done, helps cast at least some branches of social science in what is undeniably a scientific posture—a posture inviting empirical refinement and preparing to capitalize on it. The charges that social science fails as science lose a good deal of their plausibility anyway if we cease to treat science as an all-or-nothing matter. We need not exclude every inquiry that fails to be as rigorous as classical mechanics. We can instead look upon science as a matter of degree. This view, which accords better with the variable degrees of success found in natural science, too, would regard empirical science as embracing many different activities of inquiry about the world that we actually live in. It would rank such an activity as more scientific rather than less by resort to some reasonable list of characteristics. The more of the characteristics manifested by the activity, and the greater the degree to which it manifests any of the characteristics, the more scientific it would be judged to be.

An imperfect but reasonable list might include the following characteristics, proceeding from the bottom (characteristic 1) to characteristics ever more ambitious as we rise numerically through the list. As we rise, we ask in turn of any activity of inquiry that is in question:

1. Is it pursued indefinitely rather than taken up and brought to an end within the confines of one practical crisis?
2. Does it aim to decrease the stock or potential stock of false statements describing the real world and to increase the stock or potential stock of true statements?
3. Does it circumscribe a field of research and aim to fill gaps in the literature identified as pertinent to the field?
4. Does it aim to establish by generalization explicitly related sets of true descriptive statements?
5. Does the activity aim to increase the stock of true causal generalizations? (This implies increasing at the same time the stock or potential stock of true singular causal statements and the number of explanations and predictions that can be argued in some approximation to the covering law form.)

[20]David Braybrooke, "An Illustrative Miniature Axiomatic System," in *Politics and Social Life,* ed. Nelson W. Polsby, Robert A. Dentler, and Paul A. Smith (Boston: Houghton Mifflin, 1963), 119–130.

6. Does it distinguish levels of aggregation such that objects on one level in some sense belong to objects on a higher level and supply facts from which facts about the higher level arise?
7. Does it aim to increase the precision of its statements, general and singular, throughout as much of its field as possible?
8. Does the activity aim to bring its chief general statements together in a unified structure expressed or expressible with formal methods as in an axiomatic theory?
9. Does it apply statistical analysis in research designs and in interpreting research findings?
10. Does it use, to achieve greater precision or more powerful theories, mathematics beyond arithmetic, elementary algebra, and graphical analysis as found in elementary statistics or economics?

Characteristics 1 through 7 appear to be cumulative for naturalistic inquiry; that is to say, they scale. We would be surprised to come across a branch of natural science that had one of the higher-numbered characteristics in the set without having all the lower-numbered characteristics securely attained. So we have, because the list is ordered in the way given, a scale—a scale of scientificity. We need a word for this purpose and "scientificity" is (in English) a handy new one.

The use of "true" and "false" in the specifications of the scale will strike some philosophers as too free and easy. They will be thinking of some theories in natural science that postulate unobservable entities and will argue that to call such theories "true" always goes extravagantly beyond the truths that can be established by observation. Or they will be recollecting that even in natural science theories commonly reign only for a time, then lose credit. They will hold that for that reason, too, scientists are best thought of as aiming not at truth, but at "empirical adequacy."[21]

Social science, like a good deal of natural science, can carry on a lot of inquiries without postulating unobservable entities; perhaps, in spite of some possible resistance in psychology, it can dispense with such postulates forever. So we need not revise the specifications of the scale on that account. The argument from the ever-impending possibility of discredit is more compelling. However, the argument of the present book would be little affected if wherever "true" appears in the specifications "empirically adequate" or "warranted by present evidence" were substituted. Perhaps at least the possibility of such substitutions should be kept in mind. Otherwise we might discount too much the risk that what we find to be true now, in natural science or in social science, will in time turn out otherwise. For my part, I think that the ordinary use of "true"—its use by people outside philosophy—is loose enough to imply that this risk is known and cheerfully accepted.

Having any of the characteristics that form the scale is itself a matter

---

[21]van Fraassen, *The Scientific Image*, 6–40; Larry Laudan, *Progress and Its Problems* (Berkeley: University of California Press, 1977), 14, 125–127.

of degree, which could be measured from left to right when, going up the list, we reach the line for a given characteristic. Characteristic 1 is perhaps an exception, but even here an activity pursued only intermittently, by people not in continual communication with one another, might be counted as exhibiting a lesser degree of indefinite pursuit than some other activities. Characteristic 4 is more typical. Some activities of inquiry have produced more generalizations, and comprehended more of what is known about their subject under them, than others. So their profiles would extend farther to the right on line 4 than the profiles of other activities of inquiry that run equally far up the list from 1 to 10.

There are two directions of development: first, up the list; second, to the right, on the line for any characteristic exemplified at all. One activity may get farther up the list than a second, while the second may achieve more in respect to a characteristic than both exemplify. Thus they will have different profiles, as illustrated by activities *A* and *B* in Figure 2, though it is more figurative than factual in the absence of actual numerical measurements.

Some profiles will be both tall and fat. These will be found in natural science. Are the list and the scale biased then in favor of the natural sciences? There is no need to say this, and it is not intended. The comparison

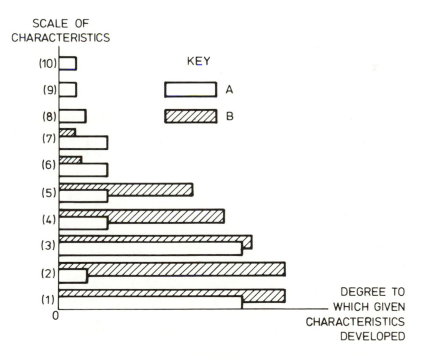

**Figure 2**

of profiles allows us, it is true, to pay a certain tribute to the achievements of the natural sciences. But is this not a deserved tribute? It is deserved even if the most proficient activities in natural science have done no more than exploit fully more favorable opportunities than have come the way of inquiries elsewhere. Nothing about the list, the scale, or the comparison of profiles implies that meteorology, with a thin profile, or comparative politics, with a profile no fatter, are not doing all that they can with data harder to come by or harder to sort out than the data of classical mechanics.

Could it be objected that the list and the scale do not do enough to bring out the distinctive presuppositions of truly rigorous science? If they did, it might be said, they would have room only for natural sciences, and there perhaps only for the most perfected branches. It might be suggested in this connection that one characteristic of science as important as any of those listed is realized by natural science alone. This is the presupposition that in the activities of inquiry which fall within science no ascriptions of intelligence, or at least of fully rational intelligence, are to be made to the objects studied.

Putting this presupposition into the list and the scale is a possible way to move in the discussion of social science. It is not, however, a move that I shall make. Not only does it somewhat jeopardize the position in natural science of certain branches of biology. It also confers, in social science, undue distinction and favor upon naturalistic inquiries. One might notwithstanding maintain that interpretative inquiries were worthwhile too, partly because in spite of failing to have this further characteristic they have so many other characteristics in common with natural science. Inevitably, however, given the normative force of the concept of science, to deal with interpretative inquiries in this way gives a misleading impression of relegating them to an inferior position.

It seems more illuminating, as well as more straightforward, to refrain in the list of characteristics from incorporating any characteristics that would preclude bringing interpretative inquiries under science. My list and scale refrain from doing this.

# CHAPTER THREE

# Settled Social Rules on the Interpretative Side

To obtain much credit on the scale of scientificity or in any other connection, interpretative social science must justify itself as being in a position to do substantial amounts of interesting work. Though less besieged by philosophers than naturalistic social science is, interpretative social science has hardly been able to take this justification for granted. On the one hand, champions and practitioners of naturalistic social science incline to believe, mistakenly, that naturalistic inquiries will expose interpretative social science—so far as it is not actually discredited as false to the facts—as nothing more than a banal recital of everyday beliefs. It is something that social science proper will supersede and relegate to the class of research programs no longer worth pursuing. On the other hand, champions of critical social science—in particular the adherents of critical social theory—threaten to swallow interpretative social science up, as something worth doing only under critical auspices. This is a mistake too. As will be shown in due course, critical social science can understand itself only if it recognizes that in sorts of questions and methods it is a mixture of naturalistic and interpretative social science. Both of these must be characterized before critical social science can be.

## RULES AS SOCIAL SCIENCE SEES THEM

As was clear from the first look at the specimen of interpretative social science found in Liebow's study of Tally's Corner, interpretative social science makes a good deal of rules—settled social rules. I have not yet explained in any detail what settled social rules amount to, much less explained how they relate to the distinction between group facts and person facts. Nor have I explained how rules lend themselves to quantitative and axiomatic treatment, enabling interpretative social science, surprisingly, to reach as high on the scale of scientific characteristics as naturalistic social science does.

What is a rule? We are certainly familiar enough with rules; in practice we understand well enough what a rule is. Yet the idea of a rule resists being reduced to any explicit definition. It is best, I think, to proceed by way of "a definition in use," which shows how we could replace one way of talking by another. Instead of talking about rules, we could talk about certain forms of words. To say that a rule exists in a given society is to say (in part) that the people who belong to that society act as though certain forms of words had been communicated to them and they had acted accordingly. It is as if, for example, they had heard the words, "If you are a married man, then you must provide for your family," and those of them who were married men had provided, or tried to provide, accordingly. Or it is as if they had heard the words, "If the government has introduced a bill and you are a Member of Parliament who belongs to the governing party, you must not vote against the bill," and acted accordingly.

The forms of words that enter into accounts of rules can sometimes be found not only formulated by some of the people who apply the rules or to whom they are applied but actually set down in an authoritative way. This is the case when we are dealing with laws as such, or, more precisely, with statutes. The definition in use says "as if," however, to allow for the possibility that no one hitherto has formulated some rules. No one hitherto, in some cases, may even have been aware that the rules existed. They may have been effective in determining people's actions nevertheless. Of course, discovering such rules is a cherished sort of feat in interpretative social science. Linguistics abounds in examples. How many speakers of English are aware until they are told that they sound *th* in two different ways, or that they shift from one sound of *s* to another when they use the word "house" as a verb rather than as a noun?

To concede that rules exist that have not yet been formulated creates a problem about their ontology (their claim to reality). One uneasily suspects that in such cases their existence may be too insubstantial to be real. However, the problem arises already for rules that have been formulated, when these are held to persist during intervals in which they are not uttered. In either connection, there are two things that can be done which, I think, suffice in principle to deal with the problem about ontology. First, the definition in use already prepares us to deal with unformulated rules by supplying forms of words by which they might be expressed. But we can translate all the talk about forms of words into talk about verbal or written tokens, which leaves nothing immaterial to postulate regarding the forms of words themselves. Second, we can treat the tokens as corresponding in certain ways to real states of affairs in the observable, material world, and to states of affairs that may or do succeed them.

Of course, the correspondence between rule-sentences and states of affairs will be more complicated than the correspondence that is looked for in the case of simple sentences expressing descriptions each of one state of affairs. An analysis of rules worked out by von Wright shows us just how more complicated.[1] Suppose we understand well enough how a simple sentence, *p*, describes a state of affairs: "The money is in your possession." Then we are well prepared to understand how a combination of simple sentences can describe a change from one state of affairs to another: Where *p* was true, we now have not-*p*. "The money is not in your possession." But then we can move on to describe this change as something done or forborne. "You are changing things (or forbearing to change them) from the money's being in your possession to its not being in your possession." Rule-sentences come next. They come in to prescribe or forbid the doing or the forbearing just described. For example, "You ought as a matter of rule in these circumstances to change things from the money's being in your possession to its not being in your possession." Rule-sentences fail to correspond when the actions are not done (or, if this is required, forborne). The rule stands. Any single failure counts as a violation of the rule. In the case of a descriptive statement, of course, the effect is quite different. The failure is charged to the statement, not to the state of affairs, and the statement is withdrawn.[2]

The phrase "as a matter of rule in these circumstances" was a stopgap for making two further points in the analysis. Rules generally prescribe or forbid actions only on certain conditions. Of the examples of rules given earlier, one was a prescription—"If you are a married man, then you must provide for your family"—and the other a prohibition—"If the government has introduced a bill and you are a Member of Parliament who belongs to the governing party, you must not vote against the bill." The prescription holds on the condition of your being a married man; the prohibition, on the double condition of a bill's being introduced and of your belonging to the party in power. Furthermore, rules, unlike simple imperatives or injunctions addressed to a single person, are addressed to many people simultaneously. Thus "as a matter of rule" the same form of words might be repeated to as many people—as many married men or Members of Parliament—as there were people to bring under the rule. Or we might take "as a matter of rule" to call for the introduction of

[1] Georg H. von Wright, *Norm and Action* (London: Routledge, 1963).
[2] G. E. M. Anscombe, *Intention* (Oxford: Blackwell, 1957), 56.

logical quantifiers so that we could say, for every person $N$ who comes under the rule, a certain action or forbearance is required on the conditions specified.

## CONFORMITY AND ENFORCEMENT

One condition for ascribing a rule to a given society is that by and large people in that society conform to it. For some purposes we may waive the condition. Contemplating a formal rule, which has been duly legislated and is still on the books, we may want to say that $R$ is the law, though it is honored only in the breach. On the other hand, we may want to say that, speaking realistically, it is no longer an effective law; it is a dead letter. When we are dealing, as social scientists often are, with informal, unlegislated rules, the condition cannot be so easily waived, though sometimes we may, as on Tally's Corner, have in view a set of rules that people do not conform to but only wish they could. Even there, an inclination to conform must be general, and in that sense the conformity condition must be at least approximated. For what sense can there be to ascribing a rule to a society if it is not something that has been legislated there and it is conceded that people neither conform to it nor care to try? The only evidence for an unlegislated rule is conformity or some approach to it.

Even so, could there not be a rule with no conformity to it? Indeed there could be; that is to say, the use of the word "rule" ranges over some cases where this is so. An example is a rule at the moment of its being legislated or promulgated, before there has been any time for evidence of conformity to develop. However, though this is an unquestionable, even central, instance of a rule, it is not a rule in the sense that I am concerned with. I am concerned, as social scientists for the most part are concerned, with settled social rules. Whether they have been legislated or not, they cannot be regarded as settled unless there is evidence of conformity.

The conformity (or attempts at conformity) need not be perfectly general. Suppose that lapses, when they occur, are decried, reprimanded, or otherwise punished, while performances are praised, or at least credited to the agents' favor. Then conformity by most people, in most cases, together with the evidence of enforcement, will establish that the conformity condition is fulfilled. It is perhaps best thought of as a mixed condition of conformity and enforcement.

In both connections, intentionality must be assumed. What is taken to be conformity is done intentionally, that is to say, the events that are counted as instances of conformity with the rule are intended to have the form that the rule calls for. This is so even when the rule has not been formulated and the person conforming to it has never reflected upon it as something governing his actions. When a person modifies one of his utterances until it sounds right to him, the person doing the actions may not even be able to describe the form that he is after. He nevertheless recognizes when he has arrived at it.[3] In other cases, he may be able to describe the form but may give it a description different from the one that figures in the rule.[4] He hires someone without realizing that once again he has conformed to a rule of never hiring a black. The remaining cases are perfectly straightforward: The agent describes what she is aiming to do in the same terms as the rule. Thus a Member of Parliament votes with her party.

Intentionality comes into enforcement, which itself consists of actions according to rules, in the same way. However, intentionality is important enough to call for separate discussion and even to be treated, independent or not, as a condition itself, as I shall do in a moment. To it may be joined a further condition of there being a society or social group for the purported rule to be ascribed to, as a rule of that society or group.

Is fulfilling all these conditons together sufficient to establish the existence of a given rule? I think we can go no further than to say that together they constitute evidence as good as the nature of the question admits. The ascription of a rule—the rule actually settled upon, even if we have a statute to begin with—is subject to the same sort of indeterminacy as the hypothesis of a natural law: Rules with different contents might be better founded. The phenomena could be categorized differently, in many ways, and one or more of those ways, once hit upon, might prove more searching and more fruitful. Furthermore, as is the case with laws of nature again, at least taken in application to observed phenomena rather than isolated in idealized models, the rule as formulated inevitably leaves unspecified a number of exceptions. The evidence will not suffice to establish the rule if the exceptions are left unspecified. Nor will the evidence ever suffice to specify what all the exceptions are.

## INTENTIONALITY

The conditions about intentionality and group basis hold most clearly when the rule in question is one that requires some reciprocity of actions among the members of a society and indeed supplies a standard form under which that reciprocity takes place. The clarity is heightened when the reciprocity is such that in one action something is deliberately signified and in the reciprocating action the significance is acknowledged as such. With some rules there is reciprocation with no signification. With others, there is nei-

---

[3]Stuart Hampshire, *Thought and Action* (London: Chatto & Windus, 1959), 96ff.
[4]Ibid., 95–96.

ther reciprocation nor signification. In the cases with richest intentionality, however, both appear.

Thus one person greets another by saying "Hello" or by waving, and another person responds by saying "Hello" or waving in turn. Or a person votes by saying "Aye." In these cases and innumerable others, the intentionality of conforming instances is established in part by demonstrating that there are specific alternative actions with different, even contrary, significance. The person conforming to the rule means to act one way rather than otherwise. He is committed to certain consequences by acting as he does, and he is prepared to have those consequences follow. He would be disconcerted if the consequences did not follow—if instead of a reciprocal "Hello" he elicited a hostile gesture, for example, or even an expression of incomprehension: "What do you mean by saying 'Hello'?" If he had meant to convey hostility, and had expected hostility in turn, he would not have said "Hello." He would have scowled or said, "Out of my way, you jerk!"

Underlying the rule and establishing the structure of actions and alternative actions upon which the rule bears will sometimes be conventions in the sense analyzed by the philosopher David Lewis.[5] Here the instances of conformity have been assigned the meaning that they have as a result of everyone's realizing that coordination on this point would be in everyone's interest. Everyone realized also that one scheme of assignment had to be settled upon rather than others. The noises that for us and the men on Tally's Corner convey friendliness might have been appointed to serve as insults, and vice versa. The convention—the scheme of assignment actually adopted to make sure of coordination—may be something deliberately legislated and may thus in its inception manifest maximal intentionality. It would also be settled upon intentionally, however, if it were established only gradually, by a process of example and imitation, though one accompanied by awareness, or growing awareness, of what the choice amounted to, in respect both to purpose and to alternatives.

With the social rules that are commonly built upon the conventions come sanctions; that is what chiefly distinguishes rules from conventions. Even failing to give an appropriate response to "Hello" evokes sanctions under a rule: It is disapproved of. The rules may be intentionally added to the conventions in either of the ways—legislation or gradual cumulation—that the conventions themselves were intentionally arrived at. The rules ratify the choices of alternative schemes that the conventions have settled upon. The rules themselves settle upon choices of sanctions. Like the conventions, moreover, the rules can be undone by human choices, concerted or gradually accumulated. A rule that one person after another comes to disregard ceases to be a rule.

[5]David K. Lewis, *Convention* (Cambridge, Mass.: Harvard University Press, 1969).

Instead of a convention, what underlies the rule, even a rule with maximal or near maximal manifestation of intentionality, may be a quasi convention. This would be something that has the effect of a convention and is equally settled but was arrived at without so much awareness. Maybe it has been taken up generation after generation as a given feature of the social world but hardly noticed as such. It may still not be commonly noticed as such; nor may the rule. Now, however, conformity to it and to the superimposed rule manifests so much intentionality that there is knowledge on all sides that the alternative actions, like the actions observed, vary in significance in the ways assigned by the scheme that is in force.

Finally, the fact that the actions conforming to the rules are meant to have the form that they take implies that on any typical occasion the action is not a slip or an accident. It may even so not be an action freely done. One may, for example, cast a vote one way rather than another because of a threat or even under physical duress. The deep philosophical question whether it is ultimately free or causally necessitated does not arise for ordinary judgments distinguishing between "done (or omitted) deliberately" and "just a slip." For ordinary judgments, slips (sealing the envelope before putting the ballot in it) are things done without forethought or reasons, though nothing in those ordinary judgments precludes their being determined in another way, by causes. Indeed, in ordinary life, in such cases we anticipate explanations that cite causes: "She was distracted by a noisy quarrel on the street below." One may want to argue that actions that are done intentionally, for reasons, are caused, too, by different causes from those causing slips. One is then arguing that there is more to be said about the actions than needs to be said to establish their being intentional. But this does not by itself cast any doubt on the procedures for establishing intentionality.

## GROUP BASIS

To what society or social group shall the rule be ascribed? There must be at least one such society or group. It would be most cogent to have just one such group in any one instance of a person's acting in accordance with a rule. Imagine having a group that was organized for certain common purposes; that was not subdivided into further organized groups; that had its own territorial base, which was not shared with other groups and not close enough to the territories of other groups for there to be, inevitably, much intercourse with them. The population of Iceland during parts of the Middle Ages might be an example. Then we would say that a certain rule for voting or for exchanging greetings was a rule of that society when all its members had from time to time occasion to act according to it and did so intentionally.

In the real world, the societies or groups to which rules are ascribed may be organized for certain purposes but, like the Society of Jesus, have no contiguous territory of their own. They sometimes, like Jews and Arabs in Israel, have their members intermingled on the same territory with other groups. They generally have a good deal of intercourse with members of other groups. This is so even when they have unique territorial bases, for members in the border regions may in fact have as much to do with members of other groups as with their own, or more. They almost always are subdivided into smaller groups that are, even so, larger than families or households, whose idiosyncratic rules are not of much interest to social scientists.

All of these matters create some difficulties for the ascription of rules, chiefly because they create difficulties about what populations shall be considered in establishing the degree of conformity in actions and in enforcements. That is not to say that the difficulties cannot be managed. The repeated success that we have in distinguishing different languages and different linguistic communities shows that they can all be managed effectively.

I shall discuss further only one of these difficulties, and that very briefly. What is the status of a rule that currently requires conformity only from an organized subgroup? Members of the general public in Canada are not required to act currently by the rules by which one signifies a vote of "Aye" or "Nay" on a bill in Parliament, or by the rule of each party according to which Members of Parliament must vote with their parties. Those rules do not prescribe or prohibit anything for them, one might say, and the sanctions attaching to the rules do not reach them. If they fail to look upon a certain gesture as a vote of "Aye," they are doing no more than failing to abide by a definition. Their error is merely linguistic and carries no penalty beyond creating a certain amount of miscomprehension.

I think it is true that the rule in such a case bears upon the general public in a different way from its bearing upon those now acting under it. However, it seems straightforward enough to continue to ascribe it to the larger group—Canada as a whole, in this case—rather than just to the smaller one (current Members of Parliament). It is a rule applying to part of a political system in which all Canadians participate. They take account of the legislation produced by Parliament. They decide whether or not to vote in the election of Members of Parliament. They decide whether or not to offer themselves as candidates for election. Should they change, within this system of which they are already part, from being members of the general public to being Members of Parliament, they would bring themselves under the conditions of the rules applying to the current actions of such members.

Sometimes, as when a certain sport is carried on in several countries, it will serve best, on this approach, to think of the rules of the sport as being at once rules, with conditions defining current players, of each of the societies involved. In other cases, as in maintaining certain international institutions, like the International Postal Union, the rules are upheld jointly rather than by parallel arrangements. Here, too, however, they can be regarded as rules of each participating society simultaneously. Here, too, the rules figure in an institutional context that connects the activities of organized subgroups—for example, postal employees—with the activities of the general public.

## RULES WITH LESS INTENTIONALITY

Even in the richest and most cogent cases, the intentionality condition, as it applies to the existence and ascription of rules, implies nothing one way or another about whether intentions are to be analyzed as having, as some philosophers have thought, special intentional objects. We do, systematically if not with infallible precision, distinguish between actions done intentionally and slips or accidents or mere physical movements. To be able to cite intentions or reasons, in the practical syllogisms that lead to action or in interpretations of them once done, it suffices to use terms that associate various forms of behavior (including linguistic behavior, such as reproof) with various states of affairs should those states of affairs materialize.

The problems about intentionality that occupy the philosophy of language and the theory of reference become even less relevant as we move away from the clearest cases of intentionality, those in which by acting according to the rules a person deliberately signifies something in order to elicit reciprocating actions from other people. Moving away, consider that the men on Tally's Corner may all sleep in on Saturday and Sunday mornings and rise several hours later than they do on other days of the week. Here there is no convention of the sort that lies behind the rules in some of the clearest cases of intentionality. The men are not coordinating by knowingly adopting as a convention one device out of several known to be available and using that device to convey something to someone else or elicit something from him. They are not necessarily trying to signify anything to anyone. Yet clearly they are all, in parallel manifestations, doing something that they could in any ordinary sense choose not to do, something distinctive in the sense that other people can be observed to refrain from doing it. (Elsewhere some people do not sleep in even on weekends.) Moreover, what they do may have some literal significance. If one of them began getting up early on weekends and going in for vigorous exercise, he might be taken to be expressing new ambition and enterprise and maybe defiance of custom and contempt for those following it. The slugabeds may themselves be expressing defiance of a society that has no use for their ambition and enterprise. Finally, on the parallel habits there may be built a rule with enforcement. The enforcement, in reproach or ridicule, may be forthcoming immediately if there is any deviation.

Rules with vestigial reciprocation—for example, rules built upon parallel habits rather than on conventions or on direct legislation—may not be of primary interest to social scientists. However, to give a complete picture of actions within a society and to show outsiders how they might participate in it without clashing with people's expectations there, such rules have to be mentioned. Moreover, such rules are not alone in opening up the possibility of taking as rules what might equally plausibly, or more plausibly, be acknowledged as natural regularities. People approaching each other from opposite directions will in most cases move to avoid colliding when they get close enough to be in danger of colliding. Is this a rule? If so it is a rule that we seem to share with ants and silverfish. People the world over do all sorts of things with their teeth, but in one society after another they generally refrain from having all their adult teeth pulled out once the teeth come in. Is it a rule (a prohibition) in all those societies that they ought not to have all their teeth pulled out? (Is it even a permission that they may leave their teeth alone?) Here we are so far away from intentionality that the notion of a rule tends to give way to that of a natural regularity. There is no need to coordinate and no convention fixing the form that cooperation shall take, much less any legislation. There is not even a standard process of example and imitation. No one looks to anyone else to see which of possibly many alternative actions will be set as an example. The question of having to imitate an example does not come up.

Yet even here we can hold that there is a place for the concept of a rule. For one thing, the regularity lies within human power to abridge; so there is some intentional sense in speaking of people refraining. For another thing, it would here again be possible for someone to signify great despair or an agonized protest by departing from the regularity. Most important of all, it may be theoretically useful for a social scientist to treat refraining to have all one's teeth out as falling under a rule. Such a rule would not, one might expect, be central or typical in the system of rules that any social scientist would wish to present as his interpretative account or theory of a given society. Yet it might figure as part of the system, for example, by setting bounds within which rules prescribing filing or blackening one's teeth represented the most extreme practices of self-mutilation. The condition of intentionality should not be used to limit the contents of theories in advance.

At this end of its range, the condition of intentionality no longer has the trenchancy that it had starting out, in the clearest cases. Yet the loss, bit by bit, of trenchancy is offset by a certain advantage. One is led to appreciate how inquiries begun by social scientists on the home ground of interpretative social science may be amplified stage by stage across a certain continuum of diminishing intentionality, moving from rules very different in conception from natural regularities to rules hardly distinguishable from such things.[6]

## VARIATION IN INTERPRETATIVE CONCERNS

The variations in intentionality that figured in the preceding discussion all had to do with prescriptions and prohibitions. These differ from conventions and quasi conventions—themselves sometimes called rules—and a possible category of permissive rules in so directly involving sanctions. The sanctions may be mentioned in formulating them. Commonly, the penalty for failing to conform is mentioned; in principle, specific rewards for conforming could be mentioned, too. The sanctions vary from being matters of life or death to trivial matters, and the rules with which they are associated will thus vary in this respect also. Sometimes conventions or quasi conventions are reinforced by having prescriptions or prohibitions, with their sanctions, built upon them, but sometimes not. This is another point of variation. Moreover, the difference between a convention, kept up entirely by mutually recognized self-interest in the absence of any sanctions, and a rule with relatively trivial sanctions attached to it will tend to be a vanishing one.

Thus rules as I have been treating them, even with my focus on prescriptions and prohibitions, will not everywhere bear upon people with a heavy hand. Champions of the interpretative view of social science may not, however, think that this point suffices to convey the importance of human individuality and personal freedom. Moreover, even when they are not insisting upon idiosyncratic aspects of that individuality and freedom, these champions often prefer to contemplate the subjective meaning of an action to the person who is doing it, leaving the fact that aspects of this meaning are shared with other people implicit. When the interpretative view does fall upon shared aspects of meaning, furthermore, its champions are perhaps happiest when not talking explicitly about rules at all. If they are led to talk about rules, as I think is in the end inevitable, they would be inclined to shun prescriptions and prohibitions in favor of discussing conventions, quasi conventions, and permissive rules. The latter must seem to leave more room for individuality and freedom. Moreover, the fact that language, the chief vehicle for communicating meaning, requires no prescriptions or prohibitions to succeed, naturally influences philosophers preoccupied with the meaning of actions.

[6]Stephen Toulmin, "Rules and Their Relevance for Understanding Human Behavior," in *Understanding Other Persons*, ed. Theodore Mischel (Oxford: Blackwell, 1974), 185–215.

Suppose we distinguish between constitutive rules, which create the possibility of acting in certain ways, and regulative rules, which bear upon activities only after they are constituted. Champions of the interpretative view, resisting my stress on prescriptions and prohibitions, might incline to class prescriptions and prohibitions with regulative rules and to think of the constitutive rules as not being accompanied by sanctions. The latter would all be conventions, quasi conventions, or permissive rules. I think this would be a mistake.[7] The out-of-bounds rule is as constitutive of basketball as any other rule. It is enforced by a penalty—you and your team have to give up the ball. If, as I agree, rules must be presupposed in performing the action of scoring, the out-of-bounds rule must be included among the presuppositions. The out-of-bounds rule, along with others, defines and creates the possibility of scoring. You cannot score by running through the stands or out of the gym to come back in from behind the basket.

In general, various sets of rules may be chosen as constituting or defining a given activity. Prescriptions and prohibitions will often be prime candidates to figure in the sets. Certainly this is so for the constitutive rules affecting voting. Despite the old-time machine-politicians' exhortation—"Vote early and vote often!"—you are liable to be punished if you cast more than one vote. Prescriptions and prohibitions are at least equally important in constituting matrimonial relations and in constituting the relations between employers and employees. They thus help constitute the activities that these relations govern.

Furthermore, meaning often rests as much on a rule with sanctions—a prescription or prohibition—as on a rule without. Would voting have the meaning that it does if one could cast as many votes as one wished? Even in language prescriptions and prohibitions have an important place, though they could be dispensed with in principle. People are prohibited from using certain forms of address to their social superiors. They face scorn, mockery, and social exclusion if they do not speak with a certain accent or do not refrain from using a vulgar vocabulary. So what they say is not said with all the freedom that conventions alone would allow. It is governed by prescriptions and prohibitions.

The clearest cases of permissive rules have to do with rights—the right, for example, of single persons to marry or not to marry as they choose. But rights are protected by prescriptions and prohibitions backed in each case by sanctions—prohibitions against interference by other people and prescriptions to the authorities to prevent such interference. Yet even here those prescriptions and prohibitions are only as rigorous as people together have intentionally made them. The heavy-handedness of prescriptions and

---

[7]As does John R. Searle. See his *Speech Acts* (Cambridge: Cambridge University Press, 1969), 36, 41.

prohibitions, when they are heavy-handed, is always qualified by the fact that they are phenomena created by human choices, which human choices can undo. I shall insist upon this point throughout. I can do so without derogating from the importance of rules and of prescriptions and prohibitions as prime instances; and without derogating either from the common, though not inevitable, fact of their persistence.

## INTERPRETATIVE GROUP FACTS

Some settled social rules are such that only groups can conform to them or flout them. Some sort of collective decision by the groups is required. Thus whether the city council of a certain municipality maintains or increases the scale on which the city makes welfare payments may depend, as a matter of rule, on whether the subsidy that the city gets year by year for this purpose from the state or province remains the same or increases. It is a rule in Canadian politics, cited by Epstein and applying to the group that composes the Canadian electorate, with effects felt by the groups that compose the Canadian political parties, that parties which do not display cohesiveness in Parliament will not be given enough seats to form a government.

Not all settled social rules, of course, mention group facts or prescribe bringing them about. But every such rule is itself a group fact. Indeed, it is a particularly clear instance of one, since the idea or metaphor of aggregation applies in a specially straightforward way. Conformity and enforcement each consist of a lot of person facts considered together. The champions of the interpretative side have overlooked this point, too, perhaps again because they were preoccupied with the actions of individual persons, thinking of them as conforming to rules in each individual case. The rules ascribed to a society, however, are not just rules that apply to one person, like the formulas of von Wright, taken literally. They hold for a lot of persons simultaneously, with direct bearing on all the members of society who meet the conditions specified in the rules. The existence of such settled rules is in each case a fact about the society. That of course is what makes them interesting to a social scientist. Whether or not any individual person does conform to them, they are there to be conformed to. Flouting them will have, because of them, some significance, and those who flout them run some risks. They are not like rules that an individual person may go on to make up for himself. As is clearest when they are prescriptions or prohibitions, they circumscribe his liberty to make up rules for himself.

To recognize that settled social rules are group facts—whether or not they are rules about what groups are to do—is by implication to concede that there are group facts as well as person facts on the interpretative side of social science. Identifying settled rules is primary business for the interpretative side. Putting this together with the demonstration in the preceding chapter that there are person facts as well as group facts on the naturalistic side, we arrive at the conclusion that both sides are parallel in having facts congenial to them on both levels.

This result—that there are both person facts and group facts on both sides—must be borne in mind in the face of the apparent asymmetry in the specimens of social science already presented. Epstein's chief finding has to do with facts on the naturalistic side, and they are group facts. Liebow's chief concern is with facts on the interpretative side, and he focuses on person facts, about persons conforming to or deviating from rules rather than on the rules themselves. This apparent asymmetry will be found in most of my further examples, with some justification in the fact that in most branches of social science naturalistic inquiry does happen to deal primarily with group facts, while interpretative inquiry concentrates upon person facts. The asymmetric impression given by my examples is justified also as a means of redressing the disregard for group facts, and of naturalistic group facts in particular, that has been a characteristic failing of some of the champions of interpretative social science. Yet the asymmetry is only apparent. In this respect as in others the parallels between the sides are more fundamental than the differences.

## QUANTITATIVE METHODS FOR STUDYING RULES

The interpretative side of social science lends itself to quantitative methods hardly less readily than the naturalistic side. This is another parallel between the two sides. The same examples of quantitative methods that I brought forward in the last chapter to illustrate naturalistic applications of such methods will serve again to illustrate interpretative ones. The methods originate, conceptually, as much on the interpretative side as on the naturalistic one. Furthermore, quite in accordance with the demands of the interpretative view, they bear interpretative significance throughout, though not this exclusively.

What makes Beer's index an appropriate one (what a psychologist would call a "valid" one) suited to measuring what it claims to measure? Just that it is an elaboration of what cohesiveness or party discipline is already understood to involve. Cohesiveness is something that people other than social scientists are ready to judge by criteria which they themselves supply. A party is more cohesive in the legislature the more often its members vote together, and more cohesive on any one occasion the greater the proportion of its members who so vote.

Cohesiveness thus understood is appropriately represented by Beer's index (though not necessarily by this index alone). It is also something that people already take into account, and hence something that already contributes to defining their situation and to making their actions significant. It is something significant in itself, resting on specific rules and attaching to specific reasons for acting. It has this sort of significance, moreover, for ordinary voters as well as for Members of Parliament. Canadian voters, according to Epstein, will regard an uncohesive party as incapable of carrying on the government in a parliamentary system. From this attitude arises the rule in Canadian politics according to which parties must strive for cohesiveness in the legislature on pain of losing their chances to form a government. Cohesiveness, therefore, turns out to be not just a quantitative fact that is a consequence on the naturalistic side of aggregating many individual facts about actions on the interpretative side. It is also a fact on the interpretative side, however much this aspect is overshadowed by the other.

Although the Phillips Curve is not itself—not being a rule or an instance of conformity to a rule—readily assigned to the interpretative side of social science, it does bring together a number of concepts that are already in familiar use in our culture. What could be more familiar than unemployment or inflation? What could be more familiarly understood to be subject to quantitative variation? Individual members of current societies arrange their affairs to make the best of these variations. They join as citizens to express a political concern with them, which is reflected in their conceptions of what quantity of either is tolerable.

Such a concern itself has to do with motivation and preparation for action. Like these things, the objects to be acted upon—the arrangements to be examined and maybe changed—invite attention on the interpretative side of social science. It is because people act in certain ways, under certain rules, that wage rates rise or fall. "In a year of rising business activity," Phillips say, ". . . employers will be bidding more vigorously for the services of labour. . . . Conversely in a year of falling business activity, . . . employers will be less inclined to grant wage increases, and workers will be in a weaker position to press for them."[8]

The third example of quantitative methods in application on the naturalistic side of social science was Homans's and Simon's treatment of the growth of friendliness along with interaction in "the external system." Here the presence of a familiar concept is so obvious as to be provocative. It maddens some philosophers to have friendliness expressed quantitatively. Those who attacked Homans and Simon on this point evidently thought of it as something like impudence to try to make any quantitative use of such a familiar concept, which has so much to do with what we

---

[8]A. W. Phillips, "The Relation Between Unemployment and the Rate of Change of Money Wage Rates in the United Kingdom: 1861–1957," *Economica*, New Series, 25 (1958): 283.

intimately value in our lives. They seem to have forgotten that we already think of friendliness partly in quantitative terms. Certainly we treat frequency of interaction as a sign of it. We often say things like, "I don't see much of her anymore," implying, when we could see her often if we did not avoid her or if we made some effort, that friendly relations have just about vanished. Or consider that people who never take the initiative in looking us up or in speaking to us are behaving in a less friendly way than we are, if we are ourselves taking frequent initiatives with them.

Quantitative considerations are in fact ubiquitous in our familiar ways of making sense of our lives and culture. What, for example, is a regular provider but someone who considerably more often than not brings home pay for the week or the month sufficient to support his family? This, with the statistical consideration implied, is what both the men on Tally's Corner and the social scientists discussing them understand a regular provider to be. Many other numbers are implied in the conceptions that both parties have of life around Tally's Corner: Consider, for example, what a steady worker is; a hard worker; a stable household. Consider how conclusions about the stability of a household are affected—for the people in it and for the observers, laymen as well as professional students of social phenomena—by the proportion of time one or the other of the major partners spends away from it, distracted by more or less numerous other liaisons. The criteria for applying ordinary concepts here, in judgments of character and significant activity, call for counting. They also involve primitive scales that can become fully developed quantitative measurements and comparisons.

## INTERPRETATIVE REFINEMENTS OF QUANTITATIVE METHODS

Social scientists working on the interpretative side can carry the development of such measurements further without in any way falsifying the data about significant activity that they are working with. Carrying the development further, they may be only spelling out what is already implied in the agents' own understanding of the activity. They may be choosing between alternative interpretations any one of which the agents themselves would regard as reasonable developments. Epstein, in representing Members of Parliament as finding it more to their interest to vote with their parties than not, is invoking a crude pattern of quantitative reasoning that the agents would presumably recognize as their own. This pattern, when it is applied in strictly economic connections, where agents are dealing with quantities of goods and quantities of money that they exchange for those goods, can be carried out explicitly in astonishingly subtle detail without going beyond the bounds of ordinary understanding.

In his chief book, Philip H. Wicksteed (1844–1927), a great British economist (and a humanist and scholar besides), gives a convincing, quantitatively refined account of his wife shopping in rural England in the first decade of this century.[9] He represents her as perfectly capable of firmly deciding just how much money she would pay for an additional quarter ounce of tea, having bought three pounds for the month already. Yet, he supposes, she would not find any difference between the amounts that she would pay for a quarter ounce more or a quarter ounce less at that point. He thus justifies treating the marginal significance of the last quarter ounce in the three pounds already bought as equal to the marginal significance of the quarter ounce to be added, in accordance with the differential calculus. Consumers do not, of course, ordinarily make use of the differential calculus when they buy tea. That, however, is no barrier to using the calculus to represent what they do, especially when (as Wicksteed takes pains to point out) they are assumed only to be making the discriminations that they are making already and know themselves capable of making.

Quantities attached to costs and benefits, along with quantities expressing probabilities of their occurring, are prominent in many of the branches of the theory of games. In the theory of voting, quantities of other sorts are prominent—especially, of course, and inescapably, the quantities representing the total number of votes cast for or against a given proposal or candidate. However, even in the theory of voting, ideas about costs and benefits can be attached to the prospects of losing or winning on various votes, with various combinations of allies. Probabilities, too, retain a leading place. In social choice theory—a subject developed just because of the lack of entirely satisfactory quantities for costs and benefits—quantities of simple sorts appear in the axioms and theorems, and the probabilities of certain phenomena actually occurring are calculable. For example, the American political scientist William H. Riker and his colleagues have calculated the probability that certain paradoxical deadlocks will occur as the number of alternatives and the number of voters increase.[10]

The philosophers who attack quantitative methods in the belief that such methods belong only on the naturalistic side of social choice science entirely overlook these uses of quantities. Yet the use of them expresses an interpretative understanding of the nature and consequences of having people act under various systems of rules. The theory of games, for example, springs, as much earlier did the theory of probability itself, from an analysis of real games played for stakes. The theory of games goes on to consider what strategies it is best for a player to adopt to maximize her winnings or minimize her losses. The rule under which, as I noted earlier, a rational consumer acts to maximize his net gains is a rule for a strategy, too, this

[9]Philip H. Wicksteed, *The Common Sense of Political Economy* (London: Routledge, 1933 [originally published, 1910]), 1:44ff.

[10]William H. Riker and Peter C. Ordeshook, *An Introduction to Positive Political Theory* (Englewood Cliffs, N.J.: Prentice-Hall, 1973), 94–97.

time a rule that applies with full information, including certainty about what strategy or strategies other parties to the transactions will follow. Classically formulated, the basic rule for maximizing in such circumstances and in others treated by economics is to make sure that for the last two dollars spent one on any line of expenditure, one on any alternative line, the benefits received are the same—the same increase in utility, in productivity, or in net revenue.

Is this a rule? Some social scientists—economists especially—tend to treat it as a natural truth about human behavior that economic agents, not only agents in fields ordinarily considered economic, maximize whatever they value. It is difficult, however, to maintain this position as ordinarily understood except by putting the truth beyond the possibility of refutation—in simplest cases, treating it as a tautology. Whatever people do, they are maximizing something; and that is what they want to be maximizing. If we regard maximization as something more than a tautology, then it requires observation to see whether people do in fact maximize.

The interpretative side of social science tells us that only those people are being fully rational, because only they are making sure that they are leaving nothing undone that would help them attain what they value. There is perhaps a minimal sort of rationality that consists simply in not acting in a way flagrantly at odds with what one, at that moment and in that connection, wants to do. If a person has been genuinely asking for work of a certain kind, and the work is offered her, it is irrational for her to turn it down. Notoriously, however, people often do things that accord with their momentary desires, but run contrary to their balanced judgments as to what they need and want, all things considered. They are not taking care of themselves as efficiently as they might. They are imprudent, sometimes more flagrantly—as when they are ruining their health with drink—sometimes less so. The theory of rational choice shows how imprudence may be eliminated in even the finest detail, though in practice many of the finer details have to be foregone. (One settles for "satisficing"—for getting something that for the moment will do—rather than maximizing.)[11] But rationality may go beyond prudence: Someone who wants to help others as much as he wants to help himself, or more, can do so more or less effectively. He, too, acts rationally only if he maximizes or at least satisfices.

One might want to ask, Just how did people come to adopt the rules or standards about what they ought to do as rational agents? Part of the answer lies on the interpretative side. There one could explain how the rule that people are to take care of themselves is founded on the conception that people who do not may jeopardize as "free riders" the chances of those who try to. The answer may, however, take us away from the interpre-

---

[11]Herbert A. Simon, *Models of Man, Social and Rational* (New York: Wiley, 1961), 61, 70–71.

tative side of social science. It may lead us to consider the most general forms of successful adaptation by human beings to a changeable environment, in which some of the things that they need are liable to be scarce. It may be argued—it is argued by some economists—that a sufficiently rigorous environment, with ruthless competition, compels people to be rational if they are to survive.[12] These points, however, leave standing the rulelike character of the basic conception of rationality and its link with even more obviously evaluative notions, like prudence. People often fail to be prudent. If the environment is not too rigorous, they can get away with failing for a time. In a rigorous environment, their imprudence will soon catch up with them.

## FORMAL METHODS WITHOUT QUANTITIES

Like the naturalistic side of social science, the interpretative side, parallel again in achievement and potential achievement, is capable of using formal methods without quantities. Formal methods without quantities—formal, nonquantitative social science—can readily be illustrated by bringing in, along with von Wright's analysis of rules or norms, some symbolic formulas from his logic of norms. That logic, as already set forth, combines the logic of the propositional calculus with a logic of change. It superimposes on the logic of change first a logic of action and then the logic of norms. Coming last, this embraces all the rest. Thus, $Od(pT\sim p)$, a simple formula in the logic of norms, contains elements ($p$ and $\sim p$, standing for a proposition and its negation, respectively) from the propositional calculus, an element ($pT\sim p$, standing for a change from $p$'s being true to its not being true) from the logic of change, and an element from the logic of action [$d(pT\sim p)$, standing for doing, that is, actively bringing about the change from $p$ to $\sim p$]. To all of these the final formula attaches the normative operator "$O$" (standing for ought or must): $Od(pT\sim p)$. All of these logics are formulated symbolically. All are associated with techniques for carrying out rigorous formal deductions and proofs. Among the techniques, applicable in turn to formulas of each of the ingredient logics mentioned and also to the all-embracing final formulas of the logic of norms, are those of the propositional calculus itself. Further techniques that lie beyond the propositional calculus in quantified logic (logic with quantifiers, if not quantities) could be incorporated into the system by amplifying it to admit quantified formulas (embodying the notions of "all," "none," "at least one").

With its techniques of deduction and proof, the logic of norms furnishes

[12]Armen A. Alchian, "Uncertainty, Evolution, and Economic Theory," *Journal of Political Economy* 18 (1950): 211–221.

a means of setting up theories that are axiomatic, like an axiomatic system of the logic of norms itself, and, unlike that system, empirical as well. In an empirical theory of rules purporting to represent the rules of a given society, all the propositions, including the axioms, will have empirical content. Whether the rules are correctly represented will depend on whether their existence is corroborated by observation.

## THE SCALE OF SCIENTIFICITY AGAIN

Finally, the interpretative side can carry its accomplishments, again in parallel with the naturalistic side, high up the scale of scientificity. Characteristics 1 (indefinite pursuit) and 2 (increasing stock of true statements) hold as much, and are as cumulative, for interpretative inquiries, for example, ethnographic accounts of tribal cultures, as they do for naturalistic inquiries. So do characteristics 3 (filling gaps in a circumscribed field) and 4 (relating sets of true statements by generalization). Interpretative inquiries may have characteristic 6 (levels of aggregation). Members of Parliament, as members of political parties, are subject to certain rules that lead them to vote on party lines. The parties themselves, aggregates of individual Members of Parliament, are pictured by Epstein as subject to rules (for example, the rule according to which the Canadian electorate will reject a party that seems too divided to govern firmly). Characteristic 7 (increasing precision) is widely and prominently illustrated in interpretative inquiries, which are continually making distinctions in order to achieve greater accuracy. One distinguishes, for example, between those issues put to a vote in Parliament which the government is bound to treat as an issue of confidence and those which it is not. The British parliamentary system consists of a set of rules that cries out for axiomatization, which has already been achieved in certain contributions to the theory of voting. So characteristic 8 is present or available, though of course not ubiquitous. Characteristic 10 (advanced mathematics) may be illustrated by the distinctive mathematical thinking embodied in the theory of games.

I have left aside characteristic 5, which has to do with causal generalizations, and characteristic 9, the use of statistics. One might consider revising characteristic 5 to allow interpretative inquiries to offer generalizations about meanings, intentions, and rules in lieu of generalizations about causes. I do not think that it is necessary to do this. I want to argue, eventually, that interpretative social science does in fact have characteristic 5, though it has it by implication rather than by self-description. Rules presuppose regularities just as regularities presuppose rules. These points, however, come up at a later stage of discussion than the one to which the argument of the book has now brought us. They come up only in the ultimate, climactic stage, in which the naturalistic and interpretative sides will be shown to be, in the mutual presupposition of their key ideas, so intimately interdependent as to invite us to think of social science as a unity.

That ultimate stage of the argument and even the penultimate stage, in which more primitive aspects of interdependence will be discussed, lie some distance ahead. The next business to take up is to show that the methods and sorts of questions in use on the critical side of social science consist entirely of a mixture of those in use on the naturalistic and interpretative sides. In this respect—though not in respect to its distinctive concern and to the particular questions prompted by this concern—critical social science reduces to a mixture of the other two sorts. I do not argue for this reduction to get critical social science out of the way. I argue for it in order to establish the bearing on the critical side of the ultimate and penultimate stages of my argument. In those stages, I shall concentrate upon the interdependence between the naturalistic and interpretative sides. However, whatever is said there about that interdependence will apply to the critical side, too, through the mixture of methods and sorts of questions.

# CHAPTER FOUR

# Critical Social Science Reduced to the Other Two

Critical social science asks questions that naturalistic and interpretative inquiries in social science, left to themselves, omit to ask. As normally operating social science, naturalistic and interpretative inquiries generally involve a good deal of criticism and self-criticism. They disregard, however, the questions that critical social science presses. In that sense they are subcritical—not critical enough. Moreover, as at least one branch of critical social science offers to explain, the omissions assist in the production by subcritical social science of systematically distorted accounts of social phenomena. These distorted accounts, along with similar popular misconceptions and systematically induced popular apathy, block any thoroughgoing transformation of the status quo.

The omissions thus arouse the concern that specially animates critical social science. That is a concern with emancipation—emancipation of social classes, from oppression or contempt; emancipation of people throughout society, from ideas that inhibit rationality. In these important respects—in raising questions otherwise omitted, in explaining the omissions, in supplying an alternative account of society and its prospects, in expressing a concern with emancipation—critical social science has distinctive components. They are components that one cannot count on finding even in the most full-fledged illustrations of inquiries on the other two sides. Hence it is a side of social science not like the others, which the others neglect at the peril of delusion.

Yet to clear the way for further stages of my main argument, which aims to demonstrate the interdependence amounting to unity of the different sides of social science, I wish to argue that in sorts of questions and in methods critical social science reduces to the other two sides. Experience shows that such a reduction will strike some people as taking away all the distinctiveness and glory of critical social science. That is an unreasonable reaction. Would it detract much from Stravinsky's originality in *The Rite of Spring* to point out that it is scored for essentially the same combination of musical instruments—a full symphony orchestra—as Mendelssohn's *Italian* symphony?

Examining the claims of critical social science to supply new methods and new sorts of questions enables me to deal with a number of matters important to the philosophy of social science that I could not otherwise easily fit into my argument. Most important of these is the question, to which critical social science deliberately returns a vigorous negative answer, whether social science can be value free.

## CRITICAL SOCIAL THEORY AND ITS INGREDIENTS

Not everything that might justly be called critical social science will come up in my discussion. Nevertheless, the discussion will be designed to cover a great variety of contributions, all of them belonging to the tradition started up by Marx in his critique of British classical economics.[1] The tradition includes, besides Marx himself and his constant collaborator Friedrich Engels, the Frankfurt School old and new and certain French writers who for present purposes can be assimilated to the Frankfurt School.[2] I shall treat all these writers under the Frankfurters' banner of "critical social theory."

I shall not try to establish just what the current content of critical social theory is. That, given the variety of authors that I wish to cover, the shifts in their views, and their continuing differences, is an intractable question. What I shall do is consider a number of possible ingredients of critical social theory, beginning with the Marxist critique of ideology, and beginning there with its simplest feature, the exposé of class-oriented bias in subcritical social science. Then I shall treat briefly the "negative dialectics"

[1]For example, Karl Marx, *Capital*, trans. Ben Fowkes (London: Penguin, 1976), pt. 1, chap. 1, sec. 4, "The Fetishism of the Commodity and Its Secret," 163–177; Marx, *Grundrisse* (*Foundations of the Critique of Political Economy*), trans. Martin Nicolaus (London: Penguin, 1973), 83–111; Marx, *A Contribution to the Critique of Political Economy*, trans. N. I. Stone (New York: International Library, 1904).

[2]Herbert Marcuse and Juergen Habermas have already been mentioned as the most prominent figures in the old Frankfurt School and the new respectively. The French writers that I have in mind include Pierre Bourdieu, to be drawn on later in this chapter for a specimen of critical social science; but also, in spite of his being a much more uncompromising Marxist than any members of the Frankfurt School and vigorously opposed to them in politics, Louis Althusser. See his *For Marx*, trans. Ben Brewster (New York: Pantheon, 1969) as well as Althusser and Etienne Balibar, *Reading "Capital,"* trans. Ben Brewster (London: NLB, 1970).

through which critical social theory undertakes to identify the contradictions among the explicit professions of the prevailing ideology.[3] Finally, I shall consider some current theses of Habermas's, including what he presents as an a priori presupposition, the ideal of an open and nonexploitative communication situation. One after another of these ingredients, insofar as they belong to social science, can be captured by my thesis that the sorts of questions which they raise and the methods of inquiry which they imply can be reduced to a mixture of naturalistic and interpretative ones.

## THE INTERPRETATIVE SIDE OF MARXIST CRITIQUE

One thing that the critique of ideology does is compare what social scientists aim at doing, under certain rules that express their recognized aims and their activities, with what they are doing unawares or unawares omitting to do. The critique of ideology carries out this comparison interpretatively.

On the one hand, for example, it describes anthropologists as looking for basic social norms that control and dissipate conflict. It describes sociologists, at least sociologists of the structural-functional school, as not resting until they find, for any given feature of the social structure, some plausible way of looking upon it as contributing to the maintenance of the present social system.[4] It notes that among political scientists, a commitment to pluralism leads either to ignoring unorganized groups or to postulating that they have special means of representation (e.g., through elements of the bureaucracy that take up their cause).[5] It observes the abstract character of orthodox economic theory, preoccupied with smooth processes for reaching equilibrium prices and equilibrium rates of growth. It observes also the use of this theory by economists to rationalize practical recommendations for dealing with inflation, unemployment, and the conservation of resources.[6]

In all these connections, the critique of ideology has in view actions—trains of actions—according to rules. The rules that govern social scientists, school by school, lay down what topics to take up. They determine the form, along with part of the content, that findings must be cast in to be

[3]"Negative dialectics" is Theodore Adorno's catchword for his chief contribution to critical social theory. For a clear account, see David Held, *Introduction to Critical Theory* (Berkeley: University of California Press, 1980), 200–222.

[4]The chief figure in the structural-functional school is Talcott Parsons. See, for example, his *Structure and Process in Modern Societies* (Glencoe, Ill.: The Free Press, 1960).

[5]David B. Truman, *The Governmental Process* (New York: Knopf, 1951).

[6]For a brief (non-Marxist) critical discussion, see John Cornwall, "Macrodynamics," in *A Guide to Post-Keynesian Economics*, ed. Alfred S. Eichner (White Plains, N.Y.: Sharpe, 1979), 19–33.

accepted as satisfactory. A pluralist account of politics, if it mentions unorganized groups, will describe some means by which their interests are represented. Otherwise it will not attain satisfactory closure. In economics, market solutions steadily win most favor. To economists they are eminently satisfying, regardless of matters left out of account, like the political processes that sustain inflation. For these are matters that economists are professionally not required to deal with.

Some of the rules governing social scientists are very stringent. Economists are quite strictly bound to deal only with gains and losses that can be measured in money. They are bound also to accept without criticism the consumers' preferences that are reflected in these measurements through effects upon prices. With the tacit exclusion of various criminal preferences, one preference is for economists, keeping within the settled social rules for their inquiries, as good as any other.

Economists are quite aware of what in the first instance they are excluding by these rules, though the critique of ideology will say that they are far from realizing the ideological significance of the exclusions. They knowingly exclude any attempt to distinguish preferences serving needs from other preferences. They knowingly exclude any attempt to evaluate policies by their success or failure in meeting needs, whether or not these needs or meeting them can be measured in money. If an economist, hitherto accepted as orthodox, should defy these exclusions, other economists will fall upon him mercilessly.

When the eminent economist Tibor Scitovsky contemplated carrying out a study in which he proposed to distinguish between families of preferences and weigh their merits, his colleagues actively discouraged him from embarking on the project.[7] He was on every hand denied research funds that on other topics would have been readily available to him. Of course, Scitovsky's colleagues regarded what he was proposing to do as highly unscientific. The critique of ideology is interested in just what prescriptions and prohibitions are associated with economists' concept of being scientific, because these will be reflected in what economics chooses to assert.

## EXPOSÉ OF HIDDEN AIMS

The critique of ideology does not stop with the recognized aims and activities falling under such prescriptions and prohibitions. It moves on to compare the recognized aims and activities with unrecognized aims and activities. There (on the other hand of the comparison) it points to aims and

[7]Tibor Scitovsky, *The Joyless Economy* (New York: Oxford University Press, 1976), Preface, x–xi.

activities appropriate to certain doubtful services that subcritical social scientists perform without fully noticing them, much less fully acknowledging them. This exposé is, again, interpretative work. For the unrecognized aims and activities themselves can be captured and expressed in systems of rules; and by bringing up those aims and activities, the critique of ideology and critical social theory imparts further significance to the activities and results of subcritical social science.

Refusing to take needs into account, and with them costs that cannot be measured in money, leads economists to make doubtful practical recommendations. They are recommendations vitiated by failure to give due weight to the costs of unemployment, including the demoralization that attends it and grows worse the longer it continues. Economists commonly simply assume that the benefits of reducing inflation or of accepting unlimited technological change or of participating in free international trade will in reasonably short order outweigh the losses suffered by the unemployed. They make this assumption without noticing it and without any means of making measurements that would vindicate it, in the course of recommending that free trade continue, that technological change go on as rapidly as possible, that employment be sacrificed to combat inflation.

All the while, the critique of ideology would assert on this topic and on others, the economists are (without acknowledging as much or even being aware of it) serving the interests of the people—the social classes— who profit from the present social system. In asserting this, the critique is in effect supplying an alternative scheme of aims and activities, a scheme that is hidden in various degrees and in various degrees followed unconsciously by everybody concerned. The conscious aims of economists and other social scientists, embodied in the recognized rules for their activities, fall in neatly, as it happens, with the aims that may be ascribed to the privileged social classes of maintaining their privileges. At the same time they fall in with rules that, unlike the recognized rules, can be held to mention one or another aspect of the interests of these classes and prohibit jeopardizing them: "Do not seriously question the assumption that the private ownership of the means of production is natural and normal."

Thus, topics, like the needs left unmet by unemployment, tending to unsettle acceptance of the present system will be dismissed or specially treated to defuse them. Burdens like unemployment that are not directly borne by the privileged classes will be accepted with remarkable equanimity. What social scientists will be found advocating, just as if they were consciously striving to fall in with the aims of the privileged classes, are measures that promote the interests of those classes. The rules for accepting inquiries as respectably scientific make sure of this just as if they had been deliberately laid down for that purpose.

## SHORTCOMINGS IN THE CRITIQUE

The critique of ideology cannot expect to propound its findings without meeting controversy. Expecting controversy and having an answer ready for it are different things. Even combined, the two of them may fall far short of laying the controversy to rest. I have portrayed the critique of ideology as making sweeping assertions about economists and other social scientists. Characteristically, the assertions are too sweeping to stand. They demand distinctions between cases and other careful refinements, which, characteristically, they do not get.

Not all economists, not even all orthodox economists, accept unemployment with equanimity. Not all economists refuse to take needs seriously in distinction from mere preferences or preferences not expressing needs. Scitovsky is a case in point, and apart from his work on this topic he is a perfectly orthodox economist. Other economists, too, have broken out of the stultifying ideological confines of orthodox welfare economics. This is the branch of economics that purports to show what arguments economics can furnish for recommendations on social policy. It does not discriminate among preferences and leaves unquestioned the preferences of the privileged for their advantages. Some economists have notwithstanding made a beginning on discriminations that lead to such questions. They have, for example, worked on "social indicators," trying to define adequate statistical measures for success in policies about housing, education, medical care, and many other matters. Here they have put forth some of the most useful contributions ever made to the systematic use of the concept of needs.[8] Even in Marx's time there were bourgeois economists who called for drastic restrictions on inheritance as an essential condition for optimal results from the market.[9] This was hardly a service to property owners in the privileged classes.

The critique of ideology may not succeed in parrying such objections to its simplest ventures of exposing the services done under ideology for the privileged classes. It may not succeed in making somewhat more searching points about the extent to which even the critics who arise among established social scientists keep within the bounds of the prevailing ideology. Criticisms that do not call the foundational principles of the current system into question or that are not joined with effective transforming activity if they do may even assist in perpetuating the system by making it more flexible and in perpetuating the ideology by making it look more tolerant. But this remains only an interesting suggestion until it is backed by firm, detailed evidence.

[8]For example, Richard Stone, *Towards a System of Social and Demographic Statistics* (New York: United Nations, 1975).

[9]For example, John Stuart Mill, *Principles of Political Economy* (Toronto: University of Toronto Press, 1965 [originally published, 1848]), books 1 & 2, 225.

Whether the critique of ideology succeeds or fails, its success or failure depends on carrying through the sort of program that is characteristic of interpretative social science. In the connections just considered, it has to match social groups against ascriptions of rules. It has to identify settled social rules, recognized or unrecognized, by looking within given social groups for patterns of conformity and enforcement. It has to compare rules and sets of rules and locate conflicts—contradictions—among them.

## NEGATIVE DIALECTICS

Ideology, as the Marxist critique of ideology conceives of it, is a subtler, more pervasive, and more complicated matter than class-oriented bias. The ideology of an epoch may have progressive features. In bourgeois ideology, these include the sweeping advances toward a rational conception of the world and of society extolled in *The Communist Manifesto.* They include, besides, the indispensable contribution to the achievements of capitalism made by enlisting and motivating everyone in the society to do her part while those achievements have yet to be completed. People in the privileged classes sincerely believe in the prevailing ideology, and they go on believing it, to their disadvantage, when, no longer suitable, it blinds them to impending social change. But the ideology, it may be held, has always been to their disadvantage in the sense that the distortions associated with it, like the privileges, prevent everyone concerned, privileged or oppressed, from attaining full humanity. How can you be fully honest and fully compassionate in dealing with someone deprived to maintain your privileges?

These disadvantages can be appreciated by bringing to light the contradictions in the prevailing ideology—not just the contradiction or discrepancy between professed aims and unacknowledged ones but contradictions within the professions themselves. Critical social theory identifies these contradictions by "negative dialectics"—by forcing the implications of one profession up against the implications of another. A simple example, which may be the most important of all to the Marxist critique of ideology, lies in the contradiction that it finds between the profession of equal rights to life, liberty, and the pursuit of happiness on the one hand and on the other hand the professions (also common in bourgeois constitutional documents) that include among these rights the right of private ownership in the means of production. For this right, it is pointed out, when it involves the power to hire or fire workers who themselves own no such means, carries with it the power to curtail the workers' rights on and off the job. The ideology thus sanctions drastically circumscribing the rights—and the lives—of most people in the very course of prescribing a full range of rights for everybody.

Contradictions are specially important to philosophers. Certainly philosophers are more preoccupied with them than social scientists are. Thus the systematic search for contradictions in the prevailing ideology may be something that can be traced to philosophical inspiration and training. It is still, however it originates, interpretative social science in upshot. It deals with the beliefs, desires, and intentions that people are observed to have. It deals with the rules that they conform to or fail to conform to. Liebow, who was not inspired in his inquiries by any Marxist doctrine, noted discrepancies between his subjects' actions and the supposedly prevailing rules. He went on to identify another set of rules (the rules for "macho" conduct) that was incompatible with—contradicted—the first. So interpretative social science is already concerned with contradictions. The critique of ideology and critical social theory, with negative dialectics, makes the search for contradictions more systematic and presses it in a more comprehensive perspective, taking in whole societies and whole epochs. It does not, however, introduce a new sort of question or a new method.

## RELATION OF CRITIQUE TO PHILOSOPHY

Practitioners of critique aim to discuss the concepts that govern (through rules) what people, even when they are confused, think and do—both social scientists and members of the general public. The practitioners analyze the concepts by setting forth those rules. These are concerns characteristic of philosophy. Practitioners of critique are also concerned, very self-consciously and to an important degree, with bringing to light the concepts and rules that they themselves have been governed by as formerly uncritical members of the general culture surrounding them. Thus they would contribute to the self-understanding of the culture and the society that embodies it. This, too, is a concern characteristic of philosophy.

One might well concede that practitioners of critique, working with these concerns, are doing philosophy. That does not set the critique of ideology apart from social science and its observational tasks. Philosophy itself is at least in large part observational, interpretative social science, though observation in philosophy takes a peculiar form. It occurs in dialectical exchanges. One person puts forward views of terms and concepts; the others rejoin with criticisms based on discrepancies between the views stated and their own linguistic practices. This is how philosophers carry on the discussion of "rules" and "explanations," for example.

However, the critique of ideology has observations to make on the interpretative side of social science besides those that are relevant to philosophy. Practitioners of critique are concerned in part to set forth the ideas of others, whose ideas they do not share. When they study economists and sociologists, they act more as anthropologists—ethnographers—studying people of another culture than as philosophers studying themselves and their own ideas. (Perhaps they act like philosophers studying the practices of scientists without appreciating the limited uses for this purpose of the philosophical style of observation.)

## THE NATURALISTIC SIDE OF MARXIST CRITIQUE

My contention that methods of the critique of ideology are either those of interpretative social science or those of naturalistic social science would stand if the methods were wholly interpretative. They could be wholly interpretative in the ways just surveyed. It cannot be denied, furthermore, that many practitioners of critique find interpretative methods much more congenial. This is not surprising, given the philosophical training of many of them. Yet what is chiefly distinctive about the Marxist critique of ideology is that it upholds a specific theoretical explanation of the omissions and distortions which it finds in subcritical social science, naturalistic or interpretative.

This explanation, I am about to show, is in its general framework, and not only there, causal. Hence it, and the critique of ideology with it, have an important commitment to naturalistic methods. What the critique of ideology is saying cannot be appreciated without giving due attention to its naturalistic side.

Practitioners of critique themselves, ironically, vary in this appreciation and attention. Some do not recognize the naturalistic side of their work. Others concede it only grudgingly or incidentally. However, their heroes Marx and Marx's close collaborator, Engels, who did not at all share the misgivings of the Frankfurt School about naturalistic social science, readily offer frank acknowledgment.[10] Moreover, whenever a theory of ideology—that is to say, a theoretical explanation of its origin and career—is invoked in the tradition of thought to which critical social theory belongs, it is basically Marx's theory that comes forward. That theory is firmly causal.

Let us call the set of settled social rules specially developed to govern the activity of social scientists other than practitioners of critique (in their critical capacity) the social-science governing set. The framework of the critique of ideology says that a given social-science governing set of rules exists because of the presence of a given social class structure. Were the social class structure to change, either by turning into another one or by giving way to a classless society, the social-science governing set of rules would change, too.

Like the connection between changes in class structure and changes in the rules followed by the general public, this is a causal connection, just

---

[10]Marx, *Capital*, Preface, 89–93; Friedrich Engels, *Socialism: Utopian & Scientific* (extracts from *Herr Eugen Duehring's Revolution in Science*, 1878), in Robert C. Tucker, ed., *The Marx-Engels Reader*, 2nd ed. (New York: Norton, 1978), 683–717.

one of a number to be found in the theory of ideology that critical social theory inherits from Marx. We can express it by saying that the presence of a given social class structure causes the existence of a given social-science governing set of settled social rules. Applying Mackie's terminology again, the presence of the class structure is an INUS condition (an Insufficient but Necessary condition in a combination Unnecessary but Sufficient) of the existence of the set of rules. The connection is certainly not itself a rule. There is nothing that critical social theory would recognize as a rule-following agent which chooses to match the given class structure with that set of settled social rules.

It is true that the critique of ideology wants to say that in all the cases where this connection operates the social-science governing set will turn out to be one that suits the class structure. It suits in particular by favoring at least for a time the interests of the privileged social classes (if there are such classes). The connection that I have singled out thus develops into a functional explanation. In some sense, it is held, the social-science governing set has the character that it does because it has the function of safeguarding the class structure in the interest of the social classes favored by it. I shall not go into the vexed issue about the validity of functional explanations that this thesis raises. The connection that I have singled out, which is more basic, does not itself furnish a functional explanation. It amounts to no more than linking social class structures, including the classless society as a limiting case, with different specific social-science governing sets of rules. Yet the connection is a fully formed causal regularity as it stands.

## MAINTENANCE OF RULES GOVERNING SOCIAL SCIENTISTS

Besides the grand causal connection between the social class structure and the social-science governing set of rules, there are points of causal detail to be made about how social scientists are kept following those rules. Suppose the critique of ideology has identified and set forth the social-science governing set of rules. The critique of ideology can make a number of telling naturalistic observations about the systems of rewards and punishments operating with that set of rules. I shall illustrate the observations from an article by the French philosopher and sociologist Pierre Bourdieu.[11]

According to Bourdieu, social scientists strive against each other for prestige and the privileges of prestige. They compete with special vigor for the privilege of having their own ideas and their conceptions of social

---

[11]Pierre Bourdieu, "The Specificity of the Scientific Field and the Social Conditions of the Progress of Reason," *Social Science Information* 14 (1975): 19–47.

science taken as authoritative for the current organization and content of social science. Among the fruits of success are to be found the best jobs and the greatest influence. So it will be a rare person joining any field of social science who will not fall into line with the current fashions and try to accommodate his inquiries to the perspectives of the most prominent current figures in the field. It is their approval that people have to win on the normal, favored route to success. The same situation prevails in natural science, but there, Bourdieu holds, competition has advanced so far and is so unremitting in detail that the effect of the competition is to uphold rigorous empirical standards for certifying advances in science. In the social sciences, the absence of any accumulation of rigorous theory leaves the struggle for prestige and influence relatively unconfined by tests respecting reality. Fashionable pretensions can easily masquerade as genuine science.

The pretensions, like other features of competition within the scientific community, are encouraged or discouraged by a second system of rewards and punishments. These are the rewards and punishments made available in the larger community. The people with power and large stakes in the present system want to have good things said about it. They want criticisms either muted or deflected from fundamental issues. Economists who do not raise questions about the advantages of free trade, including freedom for private property owners to export and import capital as they please, are more likely to get consulting jobs. They are more likely to be invited to air their views in the financial press. They are more likely to be asked for advice by governments that are themselves loyal to the interests of private business.

This account of rewards and punishments, I hold, sets forth causal processes to explain in detail how the social-science governing set of rules characteristic of orthodox social science is maintained. To be sure, as I foretold, the account touches on matters—approval, for example; the desire for approval; the choice of the most promising means of advancement—that are topics suited to interpretative social science. This interpretative content cannot be set aside as an essentially extraneous complication. However, the account marshals this content within causal schemes. It portrays social scientists as placed in certain circumstances where events of certain kinds (e.g., actions favorable to them) will occur only if they behave in certain ways. It asserts that as an effect of this feature of the circumstances, only social scientists who exhibit this behavior survive to reach posts of prestige and power.

## TREATING PEOPLE AS OBJECTS OF CAUSES

The causal account of rewards and punishments just given may be said to treat the social scientists under study as objects subject to external pressures. Critical social theory insists not only on noticing these pressures. It insists on decrying them. The critique is committed to emancipating people from the delusions that mask the pressures and facilitate their operation. It considers this concern with emancipation to distinguish it from other attempts at social science. I think it is correct to do so. It goes on to decry naturalistic social science in particular for repudiating explicit value-commitments entirely, while it all along is stigmatized by strong implict value-commitments adverse to the interests of many people. I think there is a good deal of truth in this. However, going beyond the Marxist critique, some adherents of critical social theory are inclined to contend that by treating people as objects subject to causes, naturalistic social science inevitably lends itself to the service of interests that would manipulate the people in question or otherwise (less deliberately) curtail their freedom.[12]

Naturalistic social science does not in fact, in its search for causes, entirely disregard the aspects of human beings and social phenomena that are of special concern to interpretative social science—and, here, to critical social theory. We have just seen how naturalistic social science can embrace within a causal scheme approval, desire for approval, and choice. Naturalistic social science does take the liberty of treating people, for purposes of particular inquiries, only as represented by selected features, which may not express the intentions of those people or give weight to their human capacity to communicate. It studies unemployment, for example, by asking how the rate of unemployment varies from one season to another or whether the average annual rate is increasing even as Gross National Product increases.

Social scientists who take no more account than this of the human character of unemployed people would give a drastically and perversely impoverished picture of them. They might by doing so reduce or divert the compassion that the producers or the consumers of social science would otherwise feel for the plight of the unemployed. They would certainly fall short of treating people with the respect due them as free agents with aims that they can justify as deserving recognition and support. Interpretative—and critical—social science give such matters full weight, sometimes so much weight as to enlist their human subjects as informants, critics, or participants in research. One may rejoice to have this complementation. Without it, if the impact of naturalistic social science had to be judged alone, misgivings about suppressed human concerns and opportunities for manipulation would be more urgent.

Given such complementation, how much should one fear that causal inquiries and causal findings will impair human freedom? With or without

---

[12]See, for example, Karl Otto Apel, "Types of Social Science in the Light of Human Cognitive Interests," in *Philosophical Disputes in the Social Sciences*, ed. S. C. Brown (Brighton, Sussex: Harvester Press, 1979), 22–24. Cf. Herbert Marcuse, *One-Dimensional Man* (Boston: Beacon Press, 1964), 87, 168–169.

such complementation, it is a confusion to think that they inevitably increase the extent to which people are controlled by causes. The confusion may have to do in part with a fear that if certain connections are causal, maybe nothing can be done about them by the people affected. This fear, moreover, may be heightened by attributing to every practitioner of naturalistic methods the position held by some philosophical champions of those methods, namely, that all genuine knowledge acquired in the social sciences is naturalistic. To this, to some more frightening still, may be joined the position that human choices are, like any other natural phenomena, causally determined, ultimately by laws of nature discoverable in biology and physics.

A practitioner of naturalistic methods like Epstein—or Liebow, who, as we shall see, is in some connections naturalistic too—is not, however, committed to any of these positions. Without prejudice to an ultimately deterministic or ultimately libertarian account of human choices, or to an account reconciling the two, Epstein and Liebow can hold that once people become aware of the effects of certain conditions that they have discovered, naturalistically, to have operated in the past, those conditions themselves may be deliberately modified.

Put another way, we can say that adding the new condition of awareness to the old conditions creates a new combination of conditions in which the old conditions may operate differently. This is one way in which causal laws in social science may turn out to be transitory. Suppose the conditions in those laws consist to any extent of unintended consequences. Then we also have an illustration here of how even naturalistic social science may be inherently critical in impact. By bringing unintended consequences to light, naturalistic social science confronts the people, both social scientists and members of the general public, whose actions have had those consequences, with the opportunity to do something about them.[13] They may choose to act differently; avoid the consequences; suspend (by suspending the fulfillment of the conditions) the causal laws. At the very least, it would seem that a causal theory of the effects of such circumstances is capable of making a substantial contribution to consciousness-raising and enlightenment. "Look!" the critique might say, advancing the causal theory, "This is what is happening to you," and then, in exhortation, point out what can be done about it.

## VALUE-COMMITMENTS IN SOCIAL SCIENCE

Some practitioners of critique might consider that to admit naturalistic methods even to this extent would jeopardize the distinctiveness conferred

---

[13]I heard Anthony Giddens make this point about being inherently critical in a conference at the University of Chicago in May 1984, but I have not been able to turn it up in any of his published writings.

on their work by their value-commitment to emancipation. They may be inclined to hold that every finding in social science subcritical, would-be critical, or critical is somehow marked, unlike the straightforward causal findings typical of the natural sciences, by a value-commitment. Either it has a healthy commitment to emancipation; or it has a corrupt, generally unacknowledged commitment to the ideology of the status quo.

Can this plausibly be maintained respecting individual statements like Epstein's conclusion that it is the presence of the British parliamentary system in Canada which causes Canadian political parties to be cohesive in Parliament? Or (to consider an interpretative finding) like Liebow's contention that the men on Tally's Corner begin by trying to abide by the rules for being good providers? One may allow that simply by asserting these things, and maybe in other ways as well, Epstein and Liebow may in effect be lending them undue importance. Perhaps neither they nor anybody else practicing subcritical social science goes on to put them in the perspective of the class struggle. One may point out with great force the service that such omissions do for certain values and certain social classes. But would it follow from these points that the statements are when taken by themselves suspect, untrue, or empirically unwarranted?

It is a fallacy to argue, from the ideological impact of a whole body of statements, naturalistic or interpretative, to the conclusion that every statement in that body, $s_1$, $s_2$, $s_3$, etc., has an ideological cast and import. Practitioners of critique would miss a dramatic opportunity to advance their aims if they lapsed into this fallacy. Avoiding it, as it may be conceded they do, they can point out that every single statement in a set of statements about social phenomena can be true, yet the whole set can have ideological, distortive consequences for people's thinking. An example would be a careful study of how a political system—the city of New Haven, say—resolved issues on a given agenda, if the study left out of account how the agenda was limited to suit people not otherwise active in the system.[14]

It is difficult to tell which—the observations of manipulation, exploitation, and oppression, or the judgments denouncing these things—come first. I expect it is idle to ask. As far back as one might get to the origins of an inquiry within the critique of ideology, one would find some suspicion, engendered by observations, about the facts being amiss hand in hand with some disposition to denounce certain facts as oppression if they came to light.

In respect to the operation of value-commitments to prompt and direct inquiries at every turn, the critique of ideology is typical of social science. Critical social science does not on this point differ from the naturalistic or interpretative sides of social science. Likewise typical is the fact that

---

[14]See the attack by Peter Bachrach and Morton S. Baratz, *Power and Poverty* (New York: Oxford University Press, 1970), on Robert A. Dahl's *Who Governs?* (New Haven: Yale University Press, 1961).

the content of the value-commitments intersects with the content of observation-statements. It is just certain facts—hard, perhaps impossible, to describe except in a tendentious way—that call forth condemnation as oppression and lead to recommendation of sweeping changes. Yet even these tendentious statements must in the end be supported by evidence capable in principle of laying to rest doubts about their factual implications. People who are in fact informed, mobile, prosperous, and happy are not oppressed, however much one might have expected them to be.

Moreover, again, the ease with which nontendentious descriptions can be found varies greatly from topic to topic. Lots of individual statements, the ones cited from Epstein and Liebow among them, are tendentious only to a vanishing degree or not at all. A corpus or system of such statements might still be charged with grave omissions, as we have seen. However, omissions alone would not disqualify the corpus for acceptance in a perspective that, allowing for the human concerns most eligible for being valued, corrects the omissions. We may properly, after due reflection on the values that we wish to choose, demand that such a perspective be adopted. Doing so hardly excuses us from being careful about evidence. On the contrary. How can we know whether our values are being advanced or jeopardized unless we look for the evidence?

## METHODS FOR FIRST-ORDER QUESTIONS

With only minimal notice of shifting from one object of inquiry to the other, the preceding discussion has from time to time treated critical social theory as having the beliefs and rules of the general public as a second object in addition to the beliefs and rules of social scientists. Members of the general public follow certain rules, including rules governing their beliefs. Interpretative inquiry identifies the rules. But naturalistic inquiry then brings to bear questions about the origin and inculcation of the rules and their susceptibility to change. Thus members of the general public follow the rules of freedom of contract in the labor market and the rules about private property in the means of production without protesting against the oppressive features of either, indeed without really being aware of those features.

Critical social theory, on the account of it given earlier, has a further object. It asks first-order questions about social phenomena in addition to second-order questions about how accurately social scientists on the one hand and members of the general public on the other have informed themselves about those phenomena. Sometimes the two sets of questions, first-order and second-order, are difficult to tell apart. Indeed, they intersect, as they do in the examples just given of freedom of contract and of private property in the means of production. What people do about these things is inseparable from what they believe about them, and vice versa. That they believe in respecting contracts freely made shows in their not interfering with them. But this intersection is expectable, given the fact that the theoretical framework which critical social theory employs to explain features of social science and of public opinion rests on an account of basic social processes in which every member of the society is involved.

Separable or inseparable, the first-order questions that critical social theory pursues call for the same mixture of methods as the second-order ones. To return to the bus incident with which this book began, the questions about the bystanders' feeling so little responsibility and not being willing to abide by the rules of the market were first-order questions. Both interpretative and naturalistic questions can be got out of them: interpretative questions about how the rules that the bystanders actually follow fit in with the rules ideologically professed in their society; naturalistic questions about how and where provisions for training people in the professed rules lapsed, and how the discrepancies between professed rules and actual rules came about.

## THE TWO SIDES OF MARXISM

My reductive argument or hypothesis can claim to resolve a long-standing controversy—which ramifies deep into critical social theory and elsewhere—about the nature of Marxist doctrine. Marx's disciples have tended to divide into two camps: one that treats him as a naturalistic social scientist and another that treats him as an interpretative one.[15] But he was both. He regarded causal laws like those operating under capitalism as genuine ones; and in asserting those laws he gave a naturalistic account of capitalism. But he also regarded those laws as transitory. In his theory of social change he linked the transition between one set of laws and another to the shift from one set of rules (those governing the relations of production) to another. The shift is dialectically required because the old set has become infected with contradictions. Moreover, people follow a rule according to which when contradictions appear between rules the contradictions are to be resolved, and also a rule that the direction of change shall assist technological development. Hence interpretative social science figures at the heart of Marx's theory of social change. But that theory has naturalistic aspects as well; for instance, the shifts in rules are treated as adaptations to changes in technology.

Marx's critical social science, too, has both naturalistic and interpretative aspects. It is naturalistic in explaining the ideas of subcritical social scientists

15Althusser treats Marx as a naturalistic social scientist, as does Lucio Colletti. See Althusser and E. Balibar, *Reading "Capital,"* and Lucio Colletti, *Marxism and Hegel,* trans. Lawrence Garner (London: NLB, 1973). The Frankfurt School inclines the other way.

as determined ultimately by the roles given them in social arrangements that are causal consequences of the current system of production. It is interpretative in the details with which this determination works out, including the rules that social scientists accept and conform to because of their class position.

## RECENT THEMES OF CRITICAL SOCIAL THEORY

The critical social theory of the Frankfurt School has taken the Marxist critique of ideology as a prototype and inspiration for its own work. Nevertheless, on many central points it has abandoned the account that the Marxist critique gives of ideology and social science. The doctrine of the class struggle has never been entirely relinquished. However, the successes of the state in making economic crises less painful and the decline of class consciousness, especially in the working class, have led critical social theorists like Habermas to offer descriptions of late capitalism very different from Marx's description of capitalism in his time.[16]

Habermas for one points out that since Marx's time capitalism has been substantially modified by the introduction of mass democracy and the welfare state, along with the growing practice of state intervention in the economy.

These new features of capitalism have succeeded in pacifying workers' complaints to the point of extinguishing anything like revolutionary class consciousness on their part. They have enough work, and enough income from work, to obtain a substantial share of a flood of items standardized for mass consumption. When they do not have work, the compensations available under welfare-state measures like unemployment insurance and old-age pensions enable them to go on consuming without feeling anxiety to the degree formerly attached to meeting material needs. (These observations were perhaps better founded in West Germany in the early seventies than they are in northern England or the South Side of Chicago today.)

On the other hand, Habermas holds, intervention and the welfare state are devoted more to the service of the inherent dynamic of economic growth than to the fulfillment of the life-purposes of the people affected. The welfare state in particular works by measures—bureaucratic classification of clients and monetary compensation for their difficulties—that answer only superficially to the human needs at stake. Can money alone meet

---

[16]In the following exposition of Habermas's view of late capitalism I shall be working chiefly from the second volume of his book, *Theorie des Kommunikativen Handelns* (Frankfurt: Suhrkamp, 1981), 481–539. The first volume has been translated into English by Thomas McCarthy and published under the title *The Theory of Communicative Action* (Boston: Beacon Press, 1983). I shall footnote specific quotations under this title, but add "II," signifying that they are from the second volume, and "G," signifying that I have translated them from the German myself. Presumably McCarthy's translation of the second volume will appear in due course.

the needs that emerge with the coming of retirement and old age or with the loss of a job? Nor can people effectively pursue their purposes in mass democracy. Concerns as consumers and clients may preoccupy them sufficiently so that they do not chafe at the limits of their roles as citizens. However, the universal franchise gives them only a ceremony to perform rather than real control of the decision-making process and of the impact of social developments on their lives.

As things stand, at any rate, they are not using the decision-making process to resist what Habermas calls the "internal colonization" of their daily lives. The world of everyday life (the *"Lebenswelt"*), as Habermas sees it, has been governed traditionally by rules calling for whole-person commitments in face-to-face interaction. But now this world has been invaded by "the unveiled imperatives" of the state and the economy, whose representatives act like "colonial masters in a tribal society."[17] They act, in the *Lebenswelt,* to displace traditional personal relations with formal legislation and bureaucratic procedures.

In an example that Habermas develops at some length on themes close to the concerns of people on Tally's Corner, the poor and the aged are no longer treated as persons in need of help by friends and family. They are treated as clients, of interest to the welfare state bureaucracy only insofar as they fall into standard classifications for eligibility or fall outside. Other writers, beginning with the rigidity and inefficiency of the bureaucracy as an instrument for relieving the poor, have decried the effects of this change. Even if the bureaucracy were efficient, however, its coming would make it impossible for traditional provisions for mutual aid to continue or to be transmitted from one generation to another. With internal colonization, the economy and the state, themselves ever becoming more complex, "drive deeper and deeper," more and more disruptively, "into the symbolic reproduction of the *Lebenswelt.*"[18] The traditional provisions give way in the present generation; the next generation does not take them up as meaningful commitments.

It should detract nothing from the interest and the importance of the thesis of internal colonization to recognize that it, too, is on the face of it a thesis of interpretative social science. Traditional rules about mutual aid lapse. New rules involving the bureaucracy come in. To capture the thesis, taken as an ingredient of critical social theory, for my reductive argument, I need not add that it raises issues suited to the causal inquiries of naturalistic social science. Yet it does this too. Something must be behind the expansion of the state and the economy as well as behind their increasing complexity. Furthermore, something must explain why the traditional rules about mutual aid give way. There seems to be an overall causal connec-

---

[17]Habermas, *Communicative Action,* II, G, 522.

[18]Habermas, *Communicative Action,* II, G, 539.

tion, implied by Habermas, between the expansion of the subsystems and the disintegration of the traditional rules. Those rules disintegrate under the impact of the expanding subsystems. Even if this is taken as a metaphor, it evidently stands for real causal processes of sorts interesting to naturalistic social science.

While the systematic practices and rules of the state and the economy have been pushing ever farther into the *Lebenswelt,* the class struggle has been shifted out of it into the ever more formally organized system of the state and the economy taken together. There, though conflicts (for example, about wage rates and working conditions or about the distribution of government subsidies to industry) still come up, they do not take a "class-specific" form. The class struggle has become anonymous; it works on, but below the surface of current issues of social policy. It has lost its power to engender for the working class or any other a coherent view of social issues rooted in the *Lebenswelt* and daily experience. Therefore, Habermas holds, "the Marxist theory of class-consciousness has lost its empirical reference."[19]

In this connection, Habermas propounds another thesis, the thesis of "fragmented consciousness." The false consciousness of ideology has given way under late capitalism to an outlook that is not unified enough to count as an ideology or as a rival to one. Even the one form of class consciousness—the systematic revolutionary outlook of the proletariat—that might have been held to escape being false, has faded out. Ideology is not fostered, but forestalled. People who formerly worked under capitalism and supported it—or opposed it—with articulate, systematic convictions, now get along without convictions. They expect continual social change and simply hope to keep up with it. They leave vital social questions to the "experts." They fit themselves into the classifications of their skills and powers and into the jobs that the economy specifies for them. Off the job, their minds are divided, along with their aims, between their role as consumers and their role as clients. The critique of ideology thus has become obsolete, with no unified view, true or false, to work upon.[20]

My argument that critical social science consists (putting its value-commitments aside) of nothing but naturalistic inquiries or interpretative ones goes through nevertheless for the thesis of fragmented consciousness understood in the sense of forestalled ideology. In the thesis, Habermas is contending that certain rules by which people thought and acted when they interpreted social phenomena have lapsed entirely or ceased to be generally held. People no longer, for example, think or act as if they think the market, left to itself, can be trusted to provide a job for everybody willing to work. Habermas contends besides that no rules replacing the

---

[19]Habermas, *Communicative Action,* II, G, 517.
[20]Habermas, *Communicative Action,* II, G, 511–512, 520–521.

old ones have won general acceptance. This is clearly itself an interpretative thesis. To make my point, I need not add that it is associated with causal implications on the naturalistic side of social science. Indeed it is difficult again to find in Habermas's text any specific causal theses. Yet he evidently believes that this fragmented situation with respect to rules reflects changes in technology and the subsystems of social organization. There one might expect to find a causal basis for fragmented consciousness. It is enough to reduce an inquiry in critical social science to one or the other of the other two sides to show that it is interpretative. We need not, however, give up the contention that in this case as in others it is both, interpretative and naturalistic as well.

## THE IDEAL SPEECH-SITUATION

In the same way that the thesis of internal colonization and the thesis of fragmented consciousness have been shown to illustrate the use by critical social theory of a mixture of interpretative and naturalistic inquiries, further features of Habermas's account of late capitalism could be captured. Only one feature, not yet discussed, looks as though it would resist reduction. This, the final possible ingredient of critical social theory that I shall consider, is the ideal of a speech-situation in which perfectly transparent communication between fully rational agents takes place. In such a situation, no one says anything with ulterior motives; no one distorts what she has to say with the aim of deceiving other people and profiting from their deception; everyone is ready to respect other people's quest for truth, for self-understanding, for personal fulfillment.

The ideal speech-situation plays the part for critical social theory left vacant when Marx's "objective teleology" was given up. Marx thought that history was moving inexorably toward the establishment of a society in which ideology would vanish along with social classes and in which social institutions would at last be entirely suited to human beings and rational standards. Habermas's ideal speech-situation resembles such a society, without any guarantee that history is going to establish it. Habermas follows Marx in invoking the standards of such a society as the standards for criticizing current society and current social science.[21]

In these two connections, with society the target of critique on the one hand and social science the target on the other, the ideal speech-situation illustrates in a specially impressive way how considerations of value and descriptive inquiries work together. Here an elaborate philosophical construction from ethical theory (combined with the philosophy of language) figures among the considerations of value. The construction may make

---

[21]Held, *Critical Theory*, 398–399.

an enormous difference to the depth of the inquiries that it helps inspire. It may lead those inquiries on the one hand to the contention that only when the class-struggle has been resolved will people escape from the cultural impoverishment and systematic repression caused by internal colonization and reflected in fragmented consciousness. On the other hand, it may insist that not only must the descriptive truths produced by social science be certifiable as such by open discussion ending in agreement. The truths must fit into a comprehensive view of possible social developments, including those that would advance toward social arrangements in which a general social consensus would be achieved.

Yet these points do not imply that in these two connections the ideal speech-situation offers any new challenge to the reductive argument. That argument allows for differences in concerns and for the importance to critical social theory of a specific concern with emancipation. It does not deny that philosophy may be called in to formulate the concerns systematically and to justify them. It can maintain that in the present two connections, the naturalistic and interpretative sides of social science must be looked to for the evidence that the ideal speech-situation is feasible; that it answers to what even now human beings long for when they are well informed and reflective; that some social developments would advance more quickly toward it than others; that these developments could not take place without specified changes in settled social rules; that the rules prevailing in the ideal situation itself would differ from present rules and that the situation once arrived at would endure if specified precautions were taken. Without evidence of all these kinds, the ideal speech-situation could not reasonably be offered as a goal of social transformation. Furthermore, its relevance as a standard for criticizing current society and current social science would become doubtful.

It is in a third connection that the ideal speech-situation may present a special challenge to the reductive argument. Habermas contends that it must be presupposed a priori in all communications between human beings, even when these are in fact distorted. Hence it must be imputed to the people under study by every inquiry that takes full account of the complex communicative capacity and complex communicative activity that are distinctive of human beings. But every inquiry that does this—and, we may add, even inquiries that do not—must make the presupposition for itself, since every inquiry is itself an instance of communicative activity.

Is this presupposition something that can be arrived at within social science, conceived as a mixture of naturalistic and interpretative inquiries? One might well hold that it could be. It might be arrived at as a finding about what people engaged in communication would testify to, at any rate testify to after imaginative and persistent questioning. Or it might be introduced as a postulate of a systematic empirical account of various systems of rules or conventions, most expectably an account of the rules or conventions of a language. The postulate in question is one that would figure in accounts of other languages, too. When they communicated, people would be conforming to—or flouting—rules that could be traced back to a rule or postulate that prescribed fully transparent communication.

Habermas by no means seems ready to abandon empirical grounds for the presupposition of the ideal speech-situation. The commitment to advancing knowledge, including the knowledge of moral truths, that is at stake in the presupposition is, Habermas says, "naturalistically grounded" and related to the material conditions in which the historical development of the species has occurred.[22] Moreover, the particular empirical grounds that I have mentioned—first, a finding from testimony; second, a postulate of empirical accounts of language—run together with considerations that Habermas brings up time and again in his own discussions of the ideal speech-situation.[23]

On the other hand, Habermas insists that the presupposition is a priori. Habermas was once inclined to use the term "transcendental" as well as "a priori." "Transcendental" falls in nicely with the connection genuinely intended between the "critique" of critical social theory and the "critique" of the critical philosophy of Immanuel Kant (1724–1804). However, Habermas never wanted to be stuck with all of the baggage inherited with the term "transcendental" from Kant. Backing away from the term, Habermas called, to begin with, for reconstructing the theory of what is transcendental. He went on to suggest that the term "quasi transcendental" might serve better than the traditional one. I do not want to go into the details of Habermas's discussion of this issue.[24] I just want to consider the possibility, which Habermas himself might wish to disavow, that the presupposition of the ideal speech-situation is to be established by something like what Kant called a transcendental argument. Even a half-hearted suggestion that critical social theory may include such an argument is enough to raise a challenge to my view that critical social theory is a mixture of interpretative and naturalistic inquiries.

"Transcendental" signifies not only something extraordinary, beyond the reach of ordinary observation, but something that someone studying a system of thought from outside it would agree sets bounds to the system. Kant sought to explain, by identifying from inside the transcendental conditions of the knowledge that culminates in natural science, within what limits such knowledge was possible.[25] Critical social theory, similarly, seeks to

[22]Held, *Critical Theory*, 255, citing Habermas, *Knowledge and Human Interests*, trans. Jeremy J. Shapiro (Boston: Beacon Press, 1971).

[23]Habermas, "What Is Universal Pragmatics?" in his *Communication and the Evolution of Society*, trans. Thomas McCarthy (Boston: Beacon Press, 1979), 24–25; cf. his "A Postscript to *Knowledge and Human Interests*," *Philosophy of the Social Sciences* 3 (1973): 160.

[24]Held, *Critical Theory*, 325, citing Habermas, "A Postscript," 165; for Habermas's doubts about the term "transcendental" see "What Is Universal Pragmatics?" cited in the previous footnote, 21–25.

[25]Immanuel Kant, *The Critique of Pure Reason*, trans. Norman Kemp Smith (New York: Humanities Press, 1950).

establish the limits to which the inquiries of social science can be pursued. At the same time it is to set forth the conditions or postulates on which the intelligibility of those inquiries depend. Otherwise it will pretend, on its own part and on the part of social science, to know things that cannot be known and will miss, without the guidance that the postulates have to offer, the deepest truths accessible to it. Thus in critique, critical social theory seeks to discover fundamental truths about the standards and limits that explain to what extent social science is possible.

Is a priori presupposition of the ideal speech-situation, which is thought to embody such truths, something then that is arrived at and established by a transcendental argument? Such an argument, on the model of the transcendental arguments offered by Kant for his transcendental conditions, would be one that shows somehow that if one did not concede its truth one would be conceding the unintelligibility both of communicative activity and of social science as an inquiry directed upon such activity. Perhaps one would be entangled in irresolvable paradoxes otherwise. It is not clear to me that Habermas or anyone else has offered such an argument, distinct and separate from an argument on empirical grounds. But suppose that critical social theory does produce and perfect a transcendental argument which, unlike Kant's, convinces everybody who gives it serious attention. What would be the impact of this feat upon the reductive argument of this chapter?

Arrived at by a transcendental argument, the presupposition of the ideal speech-situation that social science must make for itself would not, it may be conceded, belong to the empirical results of social science. It would not belong as a naturalistic result. It would not belong as an interpretative one. So, if one accepts it and believes that it depends at least for its full force on a transcendental argument, one may say that it is thus far a possible ingredient of critical social theory that escapes my argument for reduction. However, one may equally well say that it is an ingredient of philosophical understanding that does not belong to social science. So far as critical social theory is social science rather than philosophy it reduces in methods and sorts of questions to a mixture of naturalistic and interpretative social science.

As regards the division of social science, setting aside critical social theory itself, moreover, the introduction into social science of the presupposition even by a transcendental argument leaves everything the same. The presupposition does not favor one side against the other. It is of most importance to the interpretative side, where, if true, it defines the basic orientation of interpretative inquiries. Yet it says nothing for or against the naturalistic side. It does say something about communication among naturalistic social scientists. However, this itself is a fit subject for interpretative social science, as was illustrated in applications of the critique of ideology earlier in this chapter. Social scientists working on the naturalistic side, when they communicate their findings and theories, will be presupposing the ideal speech-situation. Studying their communicative activity, interpretative social scientists will ascribe the presupposition to them. None of this will preclude the naturalistic social scientists from engaging in their distinctive pursuits, searching for causal regularities for use in causal explanations.

Whatever ventures outside social science it may take, critical social theory has, as I think all its practitioners would agree, a great deal of work to do within the bounds of empirical inquiry: pursuing the critique of ideology in social science and in public opinion; exposing contradictions; filling the gaps in subcritical social science; bringing to light alternatives in social arrangements. This work, I have argued, will be carried on with questions and methods naturalistic or interpretative. In that work, furthermore, those methods and sorts of questions will be mutually interdependent—intimately interdependent—in just the ways that I am about to show hold for the naturalistic and interpretative sides of social science in general. The reduction that was effected in this chapter brings critical social science, distinctive as in important ways it remains, within the embrace of the stages of argument that now ensue.

# CHAPTER FIVE

# Mutual Support between the Two Remaining Sides

The stage has now been set for broaching the question of interdependence—an interdependence that involves all three sides of social science, though this will now follow from making it out for two, the naturalistic and the interpretative. That inquiries on these two sides sometimes go hand in hand has become manifest already in some examples of social science that defy unique assignment to either side. The system of rewards and punishments purportedly operating upon economists and other social scientists to induce in them ideologically colored views is one such example. Rewarding and punishing are actions under rules, but at the same time they fall into place in a causal scheme. The occurrence of rewarding and punishing is a condition that causally explains the occurrence of the ideology ascribed. Skeptics about doctrines of ideology, whether Marx's classical one or the one currently asserted by critical social theory, may not agree that in this case there is anything to be explained. That would make the example for them at best hypothetical rather than real. There are, however, plenty of less controversial examples of explanations by rewards and punishments. The men on Tally's Corner, like men and women elsewhere, do some things because of the rewards that come with having jobs. They cease doing other things because their employers punish them (fine them; dock their pay). Such examples would serve just as well to defy unique assignment.

## WEAK COMPLEMENTARITY OR COOPERATION?

Does the existence of such cases by itself show that there is at bottom just one social science? I think not. Such cases might amount to no more than occasional instances of intersection—interdependence on some topics that intersect with both sorts of inquiries—with no interdependence on many topics elsewhere. Now that I have cleared the way for the fundamental question of the relation between the naturalistic and interpretative sides, I want to gain more for the thesis of interdependence than a point about occasional intersection. I want to show how various that interdependence is, and how pervasive. Occasional intersection in cases that defy unique assignment would amount to hardly more complementarity than the weakest sort that we could imagine: Both sides exist (sometimes in the service of critical social science on the third, reducible side), but each goes about its business ignoring the other. They could ignore each other even when they were at work in the cases that defy unique assignment.

The situation in respect to complementarity would not necessarily change even if they recognized each other's legitimacy. In preceding chapters, naturalistic inquiries and interpretative inquiries turned out to be equally dependent on observation, and hence both respectably empirical. They turned out to be comparable in many other characteristics that are valued as features of science, including the use or possible use of formal methods quantitative and nonquantitative. These characteristics not only figure on both the naturalistic and interpretative sides of social science. On both sides, they fit the phenomena under study. Hence, philosophical reflection by inquirers on either side should lead to according the other a substantial amount of respect.

Mutual respect would, of course, encourage cooperation, but it does not imply it. It does not imply cooperation even in the cases that defy unique assignment, since researchers on each side might treat these cases wholly in their own perspective. The intersection in these cases would then be just a matter of unintended coincidence for inquirers on the one side or the other. Setting these cases aside, I shall develop another line of argument.

Let us return to the studies by Epstein and Liebow. In focus and preoccupation these studies clearly illustrate, one the naturalistic side, one the interpretative. I shall argue that within the scheme of inquiry in each case there is, however, a movement from the one side to the other, from naturalistic to interpretative in Epstein's case, from interpretative to naturalistic in Liebow's. I shall argue further that the two studies are typical in this respect. Typically, inquiry on the one side leads to inquiry on the other.

Epstein and Liebow do more in this connection, however, than illustrate a typical shift of perspective. They illustrate a crucial aspect of complementarity. Inquiries on one side always present the other side with occasions for raising questions congenial to the second. I shall argue for this point without, in this chapter, going on to argue that the key idea of each side presupposes the key idea of the other. In this mutual presupposition complementarity peaks. There it has a strength embracing but going beyond aspects noted in this chapter and earlier. It implies that in many cases the findings of either side will have direct counterparts in the findings of the other. But this is something that I shall wait to bring out in the final chapter, yet to come. Here I shall not go beyond simply showing that inquiries on each side always present occasions for inquiries on the other.

## NATURALISTIC GROUP FACTS WITH INTERPRETATIVE PERSON FACTS

Epstein and Liebow have more to offer us than has as yet drawn attention— a good deal more. Epstein's article, in general scheme and in the group facts with which it is preoccupied, is an example of naturalistic social science. However, person facts on the interpretative side of social science are represented in it, and quite congenially and comfortably so. They form another ingredient. *Tally's Corner,* in general scheme and in the person facts on which it is focused, is an example of interpretative social science. However, quite congenially and comfortably, it embraces as well some group facts from the naturalistic side. They form another ingredient of Liebow's results. In both cases the distinction beween naturalistic and interpretative inquiries is nevertheless quite clear. We have distinct ingredients working together, not ingredients defying unique assignment.

Once Epstein has established that the British parliamentary system is the cause of the Canadian political parties being cohesive in the legislature, he asks what is it about the British parliamentary system that has this effect? He gives an answer from the interpretative side of social science. The answer describes a microprocess connecting the presence of the British parliamentary system with the cohesiveness of the Canadian political parties. The description runs in terms of the rules by which the British parliamentary system operates. Some of the rules apply to the parties in Parliament. Other rules apply to the individual Members of Parliament who belong to the parties. The government of the day must call an election if it loses a vote in the House of Commons on any important issue. That is a rule applying to the party in power. It has consequences that lead to individual members' conforming to rules applying to them.

If Members of Parliament belonging to the governing party fail to vote with the government and their party, they risk a dissolution of Parliament and the expenses, together with the uncertainties, of having to campaign to retain their seats. Epstein assumes that the Members will deal with this risk rationally. Appreciating that their own interest lies in keeping their party in power—when it is in power—Members belonging to the majority party will vote with it to safeguard themselves from the disadvantages of an election. To touch in a preliminary way upon a complex subject to which I shall have to return, each Member can be represented as dealing with the situation by following a rule defining rationality. The rule, which again may be thought of as supplying the major premise in a practical syllogism, may be expressed thus: "One should act in the way that is most in one's interest." The minor premise here would be, "It is most in one's interest to vote with one's party." The conclusion is, "One should vote with one's party." The minor premise itself can be represented as a conclusion from reasoning about the situation, as defined by the overall rules of the British parliamentary system.

This practical syllogism is itself set up as a consequence of the rule, about losing on an important issue, that applies to the party in power. That is, logically, where the minor premise comes from. But if every Member of Parliament who belongs to the governing party reasons in the same way and acts accordingly, there is a further consequence, logically implied and empirically observable: A regularity manifests itself of Members voting with their parties. This regularity will in turn become associated with a rule applying to individual Members. For it will not be left to individual Members to decide for themselves how to vote. They may on occasion be inattentive or irrational. They may have special reasons of their own for deviating. It will be important to other Members that deviations be checked. Other Members will enforce a rule of voting with the party.

The same rule emerges by a similar process from another rule applying to the parties in Parliament. Parties that do not demonstrate cohesiveness will be judged by the electorate not to be capable of running the government. The opposition parties are as much bound by this rule as the party in power. This rule is, according to Epstein, the chief consideration that leads members of the opposition parties to conclude that they should vote with their parties and to conform to a rule calling specifically for them to do so.

If Epstein's attribution of the cohesiveness of Canadian parties to the presence of the British parliamentary system in Canada rests on this microprocess belonging to interpretative social science, can it be a genuine causal attribution? Nothing in the definitions of cause that I have been using prevents them from applying to group facts founded upon interpretative person facts. Von Wright's definition, for example, already cited in Chapter 2, runs: "$p$ is a cause relative to $q$," he says, "and $q$ an effect relative to $p$, if and only if by doing $p$ we could bring about $q$ or by suppressing $p$ we could remove $q$ or prevent it from happening." If Epstein is right about the difference that the British parliamentary system makes to Canadian politics, the British parliamentary system is a cause in just this sense, not to mention others, like being at least an INUS condition. If Canadians suppressed the British parliamentary system in favor of the American system of separated powers and elections only at fixed intervals, Epstein implies, in the causal generalization that his finding about Canada entails, Canada would not have cohesive political parties. On the other hand, any country that wants to have cohesive political parties can produce them by instituting the British parliamentary system. (That itself, of course, means fulfilling a lot of conditions, which may be hard to do.)

In Liebow's book about Tally's Corner, the naturalistic side of social science may claim as its own his ultimate explanation of the phenomena that he describes in interpretative terms. Why do the men on Tally's Corner fail by one set of rules and have to accommodate themselves somehow to the failure? Some social scientists have argued that there is a "culture of poverty" that transmits from generation to generation a different set of rules from those prevailing in other strata of society. Liebow argues instead that the fundamental cause is the fact, a group fact about American society, that there is a grossly insufficient number of steady jobs available to those men which will pay them enough to be regular family providers. Here the microprocess not only fills out an explanation arrived at within the sphere of group facts. It supplies the evidence. Liebow finds that the men are, or at least begin by being, as much attached to the rules of respectable family life as men in any other social stratum. They try to live up to them. But they cannot find the jobs that they need. Only after struggling hard for some years do they fully admit defeat and sink into despair. "The son goes out and independently experiences the same failures, in the same areas, and for much the same reasons as his father. What appears as a dynamic, self-sustaining cultural process is, in part at least, a relatively simple piece of social machinery which turns out, in rather mechanical fashion, independently produced look-alikes. The problem is how to change the conditions which, by guaranteeing failure, cause the son to be made in the image of his father."[1]

The basic causal statement here is one in which a naturalistic group fact figures alongside an interpretative person fact. The group fact, put together from facts about individual employers and job offers present or absent, is the scarcity of decent jobs. The person fact is the failure of some given black man on Tally's Corner in his attempt to become a regular provider. More precisely, it might be said that we have in view a family of causal statements, in each of which the same group fact about the scarcity of jobs figures along with a fact about the failure of an individual person, a different person as we change from statement to statement. Mixed statements of this sort are as legitimate in social science as statements wholly

---

[1]Elliott Liebow, *Tally's Corner* (Boston: Little, Brown, 1967), 223.

about group facts or as statements, general or particular, wholly about person facts.

## INTERPRETATIVE GROUP FACTS WITH NATURALISTIC PERSON FACTS

Since there are group facts and person facts on both sides, one would expect to find combinations that are the reverse of those just considered; and we do. We can find instances in which the group facts are interpretative, not naturalistic, and the inquiry moves from establishing them to considering what naturalistic person facts account for their origin and persistence. I shall have more to say about the general possibility of such instances in a moment, when I begin arguing that complementarity of this kind is typical and always potential. Here I shall just say enough, in the form of generally illustrative remarks, to bring out the symmetry and the nature of the reverse combinations.

Consider, again, that rules are group facts even when they are not rules that groups alone can conform to. They are, moreover, certainly interpretative group facts. Discovering them and formulating them is the chief preoccupation of interpretative inquiries in ethnography and elsewhere. Once they have been found, however, is it not natural to ask how the people involved—whether acting for themselves or acting collectively—were trained to do the actions that conform or generate conformity? Were they, for example, directly conditioned to do these actions? How early did the conditioning begin, and how rigorous was it? These questions bring to light naturalistic person facts, about persons being reinforced positively or negatively in various specific ways—by being nursed and cuddled or spanked and sent upstairs.

Questions about imperfections in the training bring to light the same sorts of things. The training may have overshot the mark, so that, for example, mismanagement of the "anal" phase of a child's development leads to an adult as compulsive as King Frederick William I of Prussia (1688–1740). Frederick William, who "washed himself and changed his uniform five times a day," was even harder on his subjects and his family, imposing discipline overdone to the point of sadism.[2] Or the training may undershoot, so that, after a childhood in which no restraints on behavior were brought to bear, people prove incapable as adults of working steadily in any organized scheme of cooperation. Just what effects in adult character the occurrence of disciplinary measures or other measures of social training

[2]Peter Loewenberg, "History and Psychoanalysis," *International Encyclopedia of Psychiatry, Psychology, Psychoanalysis and Neurology* (New York: Van Nostrand Reinhold/Aesculapius, 1977), 5: 367.

have is clearly a topic for naturalistic social science. Clearly, moreover, it bears upon the question of how stringent the rules can be that those adults conform to in any given degree and the tandem question of how much conformity can be expected from them to rules of any given stringency.

## MUTUAL SUPPORT AND STIMULATION

Even if the conjunction of naturalistic and interpretative inquiries that can be found in Epstein's and Liebow's work were relatively infrequent, it would still represent an important advance over weak complementarity. Besides the parallels in distribution of person facts and group facts, besides the parallels in conscientious observation and other standards of scientificity, on occasion at least, these examples tell us, inquiries in the one perspective move to the boundaries of the other and hand over the work. With Epstein and Liebow, the shift in perspective goes through so easily that in each case it occurs in the person of one and the same inquirer, who takes no special notice of it.

Epstein and Liebow do not just illustrate the presence in social science of occasional opportunities for shifting perspectives. Their work is typical in illustrating how naturalistic inquiries and interpretative ones support each other by exchanging information. The two sides of social science are time and again complementary in the quite strong sense that one investigates matters which the other accepts as data.

Members of Parliament vote one way or another and in voting act with a significance imparted by the rules under which they act. Employers offer work on certain terms. Their offerings and the terms entailed by the offerings fall under rules defining jobs and employment. The naturalistic group facts about the cohesiveness of political parties and about the number and variety of jobs available with which Epstein and Liebow were respectively concerned rest upon interpretative person facts of this kind about voting and job offers. Thus the interpretative side furnishes data for the naturalistic.

The traffic goes in the other direction, too. Liebow is concerned with the actions and reasons manifest in the loose and fitful commitment to jobs of the men on Tally's Corner. He portrays their actions and reasons in this connection as reactions and adaptations to the group fact about the scarcity of adequate jobs. Epstein takes the great distance over which the Canadian population is spread, from sea to sea, as a group fact making for diversity of opinions in the electorate and in Members of Parliament. Most Members would vote otherwise upon any sequence of legislative issues if this factor had unobstructed weight. Thus the interpretative side receives and applies data from the naturalistic.

This sort of exchange has been going on from time immemorial without any recourse to professional social science. When the British House of Commons was rebuilt after the Second World War, Churchill insisted that it be built again too small to seat all the Members of Parliament. He said a sense of excitement, of great moment and significance, was created when every Member turned out for an issue and many had to stand while it was debated.[3] Similarly, people have long been aware that if a lot of people are competing for something valuable—like jobs—available only at the discretion of a few other people, maybe only one, the latter can expect to get more out of any of them than would otherwise be the case. In other words, the prevailing price (in other goods or services) will be higher. But a prevailing price is not a fact about any individual person. It is a group fact, like the number of people competing. Often it is not a fact that anyone intends to bring about. It has to be accepted, like rain at harvest time. It has the same sort of causal impact, even though, unlike the rain, it results from human actions that are themselves intended and done for reasons.

## UNINTENDED CONSEQUENCES

Unintended consequences like the group fact about higher prices form a category that serves as the main allowance for naturalistic social science conceded by those champions of interpretative social science who are ready to concede any allowance for it at all.[4] It is a category that will demand attention when I get on to arguing that it is not just typical of findings on the naturalistic side of social science that they offer occasions for interpretative inquiry. The occasions are always there, matters for potential inquiry, whether or not the interpretative side takes them up.

But the category of unintended consequences also has a part to play in the connection running the other way, which I shall treat first. The findings of the interpretative side of social science always—not just typically—offer matters of potential inquiry for the naturalistic side. Once again, I take the discovery of rules to exemplify the findings of the interpretative side. The naturalistic side always has in such findings occasions for asking what causes operated in the origin of the rules. Among the causes will be unintended group facts arising as unintended overall consequences of interpretative person facts.

These unintended consequences will often come in the company of natural events and circumstances that serve as concurrent causes of rules. The

[3]Charles McMoran Wilson, Baron Moran, *Winston Churchill: The Struggle for Survival, 1940–1965* (taken from the diaries of Lord Moran) (London: Constable, 1966), 122–123.

[4]J. Donald Moon, "The Logic of Political Inquiry: A Synthesis of Opposed Perspectives," in *Handbook of Political Science*, ed. Fred Greenstein and Nelson W. Polsby (Reading, Mass.: Addison-Wesley, 1975), 131–228.

joint impact of these things leads human beings to adopt rules for dealing with them. Thus there are rules—social policies—intended to prevent the prices of necessities from rising out of the reach of the poor. Among them are rules anticipating ruined harvests and seeking to soften their impact. Joseph's advice to Pharaoh to establish granaries for carrying over the surpluses of fat years for distribution during lean ones led to a rule that dealt with both kinds of difficulties at once. In such cases, experience with unintended consequences of interpretative person facts—multiple bids, for example, to purchase scarce grain—and hence past instances of such consequences figure among the causes of the existence of the rules.

Cases of this sort can be found on every hand. Letting all the members of an asssembly speak as much as they would like to on any subject has the consequence, unintended by any individual speaker (apart from filibusters), of making it impossible to get on to other business in what most members would agree is due time. Naturalistic inquiry would cite this complex fact, in which the unintended consequence is an element, as figuring among the causes of rules for rationing debating time. Such rules are commonly found in legislatures. So are the rules for bringing debate to an end with closure. Both kinds of rules are adopted following experience with unintended consequences. The rules originate as effects of circumstances in which the problems created by such consequences are liable to be renewed.

Interpretative social science will be centrally interested in the conception that people have of such problems and in the content of the rules that people proceed to adopt, understanding them to be suited to solving the problems so conceived. Must it not recognize, however, that the rules are adaptations—perhaps successful, perhaps not—to circumstances? As adaptations they must be discussed naturalistically and causally. To be sure, naturalistic social science, for its part, centrally interested as it may be in the variation of rules with circumstances and in the comparative success of some rules as against others, cannot understand what the problems are without understanding how they are taken as occasions for adopting rules. Nor could it compare rules without understanding their content.

Where do rules come from? If they were all innate, so that variations in people's circumstances made no difference to having them or not having them, they would all be effects of natural causation; and hence still caused. The attack on causal explanations in social science might, rejecting as causes anything into which human actions entered, carry far enough to imply that all causes operating upon human beings operate in natural processes unaffected by human designs. To go this far might impair our confidence in human freedom and in the importance of human choices more than any concession that there are causes of rules to be found in processes where human designs do figure. But there is no reason to go that far.

The rules cannot all be innate, since some of them satisfy a strong intentionality condition. About them, and about other rules, too, it is entirely appropriate to ask, What in the circumstances led people to adopt just those rules when they did? And wherever this question comes up, inquiries on the naturalistic side of social science are invited.

## OTHER CAUSES OF RULES

Some of the conditions operating, contingently and intermittently, to cause rules, occupy the same ground as the intentionality condition itself. Suppose we do not follow (as I am inclined to do) those writers for whom wants and desires and the having of reasons—in short, intentions, like the intentions of particular people conforming to particular rules—operate as causes.[5] We may still regard the fulfillment of the ascription condition for intentionality as at least an INUS condition of the existence of a rule. Clearly, having arrived at a convention in Lewis's sense may serve as such a condition.[6] Without the convention, the rule or rules that come into existence to reinforce the convention would have nothing to reinforce. However, the convention cannot serve alone as a causal condition for the rule or rules. If human beings were not inclined to give moral backing or something like it to their conventions and did not follow up this inclination with measures of enforcement, no rules would be arrived at on this route. Besides being an INUS condition, fulfilling the intentionality condition evidently meets von Wright's narrower criteria for a cause: again, "$p$ is a cause relative to $q$, and $q$ an effect relative to $p$, if and only if by doing $p$ we could bring about $q$ or by suppressing $p$ we could remove $q$ or prevent it from happening." Reaching an agreement, concurring in following an example, and arriving at a convention are all things within human powers to do or to forbear.

Finally, there are causal conditions which operate in just the way that the champions of intentionality most wish to repudiate—namely, as behavioristic conditioning. People learn many rules—and with the rules what reward and punishment are—by a process of conditioning, in which other people reinforce their behavior positively or negatively. That is the way, for example, in which people learn the rules, for casual conversations, about degrees of stridency and distances between people, and the rules about forms of address. But the reinforcements themselves are carried out by people already conforming to rules—the rules being learned, and

---

[5]Richard Brandt and Jaegwon Kim, "Wants as Explanations of Actions," *Journal of Philosophy* 60 (1963): 425–435.

[6]See above, chapter 3.

also, if one likes, rules about enforcing those rules. So there is no incompatibility here between intentionality and conditioning.

Nor is there any incompatibility on the side of the people learning the rules. That these people should be aware of the reinforcements and consciously shape their own behavior to obtain rewards rather than punishments does not take away anything from the operation of the basic pattern of conditioning. (I take this pattern to be more basic than B. F. Skinner's specialized concentration upon external movements, though even that may give substantial results here.)[7] Operants that are reinforced become predictable features of the organism's repertoire. In some cases, as with the distance rules for conversation, the people learning the rules may in fact not be conscious of the conditioning. So long, however, as the condition of intentionality is satisfied, the process there, too, produces a rule. If the intentionality condition is satisfied on the side of the people teaching the rule, the rule emerges from rule-governed behavior as well as issuing into it.

Not all rules are learned by direct conditioning. There is a prohibition against members of the Canadian Parliament taking pay as lobbyists. This rule is certainly not acquired by the people who know it and follow it being subjected to a reinforcement schedule specific (however intermittent and unintentional) to refraining from taking such pay. People learn it and its full force by observing that it involves sanctions analogous to the sanctions with which they have become familiar in learning other rules. People are also motivated to conform to it because conforming is instrumental to other ends—for example, to achieving impartial legislation. One might well wish in this case to stress the intellectuality of the operations involved in drawing the analogy or in appreciating the means-ends relationship. One might say with von Wright, "Normative pressure is . . . built up under the joint teleological influence of fear of sanction and anxiety to secure the ends for whose attainment the norms are considered instrumental."[8] But teleology—here the conscious pursuit of certain ends—cannot be the whole story. Beginning (one may suppose) with notions about sanctions and instrumentality associated with rules that have been directly learned by conditioning, one must learn to extrapolate those notions to rules that are learned less directly. I shall not try to describe the process of extrapolation. I assume that in its early stages at least it is a process itself controlled by conditioning. I assume further that conditioning continues to be important until the organism has acquired something like an algorithm for extrapolation, which enables it to identify a rule and the associated measures of enforcement in advance of being conditioned to it.

---

[7] B. F. Skinner, *Science and Human Behavior* (New York: Macmillan, 1953), 31–36.

[8] Georg H. von Wright, *Explanation and Understanding* (Ithaca, N.Y.: Cornell University Press, 1971), 148–149.

## RULES AS CAUSES

Besides being objects of causation in the several ways mentioned, and hence existing only insofar as sufficient conditions of those sorts have been satisfied, rules may operate as causes themselves.

Among the effects that rules may have when operating as causes is the generation of further rules. There are at least three ways in which they bring about such effects. The first is the way in which rules prescribing rewards and punishments enter into processes of conditioning. There is nothing very problematic about that; it has already been illustrated several times. Nor is there anything very problematic about the second way in which rules operate as causes, namely, by being in some cases rules that confer powers upon people to produce further rules. Under the rules governing it, Parliament has the power to produce rules by which officials of the Canadian government and citizens of Canada will be governed. Some of those rules, like the rule giving certain powers to the Department of Revenue to lay down specific rules interpreting the Income Tax Act, will enable, indeed require, government officials to make rules in their turn.

The third way in which rules operate as causes is entangled, since it stretches over much the same terrain as a logical process of generation. In my treatment of ascription-conditions, I gave little attention to the fact that a rule may be inferable from another rule or conjunction of rules. This alternative condition for ascription has been given a great deal of attention by writers on deontic logic (the logic of rules). It is a condition more important for formal rules than for informal ones, however, since before we accept any of the latter we are, I think, more inclined to ask whether it stands on its own feet in meeting ascription-conditions. Nevertheless, it must be granted some power in explaining the existence of many informal rules too. One can reasonably hypothesize that they exist because one can say that they are deducible from other rules.

There is a sort of causal generation that can be described in much the same language: A certain rule exists (i.e., has come into existence) because the people to whom we ascribe it were already committed to another rule. The new rule, I think, may or may not be a logical consequence of the other. People may adopt it as a contingent way of promoting the observance of the source rule. They adopt a rule requiring cars to bear license plates as a means to enforcing the rule that drivers assume responsibility for accidents. But the new rule may in fact be a logical consequence of the source rule. People discourage advertisers from surrounding the war monument with neon signs. The prohibition against neon signs is a consequence of a general rule concerning respect for the dead, especially the heroic dead. The point of insisting that there is a causal connection as well as a logical one is that there is no logical necessity for people to behave logically.

For proof that rules are (in various ways) causes I rely, in each connection, on their fitting current definitions of cause—Mackie's INUS condition or von Wright's possibility of intervention. It may be of some interest to compare rules with physical causes. Both may be extinguished, that is to say, deprived of any room to operate, by human actions. We can rescind rules or desist from the activities that they govern. Similarly, we can use up all known supplies of petroleum and thereby bring the operation of certain causes to an end. Both rules and physical causes can be generated or regenerated by human action. We can set up rules or reestablish them. Similarly, we can produce synthetic fuels that will work causally like natural petroleum.

True, there is a sense in which physical laws cannot be suspended by human agency. The law that petroleum is combustible will remain true even when for want of any petroleum it will no longer have any instances. But this is not so different from a rule, which has not been suspended or rescinded, no longer having any instances. Were the conditions for its holding restored, the instances would start up again. Among those conditions might be just engaging again in the activities that the rules govern, for example, reviving tournaments with jousting. One point of difference does remain: Once rescinded, a rule will not apply again until the condition of its being set up by human agency is again fulfilled. This condition, which applies to the origin of a rule in the first place, is not paralleled on the side of physical causes. Undiscovered petroleum is combustible all along. But this difference, in the face of the parallels cited and the conformity to the definitions, does not seem to require that we deny rules the title of causes.

## INTERPRETATIVE ASPECTS OF REGULARITIES

The causal aspects of rules present occasions for a variety of naturalistic inquiries. The complementarity of the naturalistic and interpretative sides of social science permits equally full illustration of reverse stimulation. Regularities have interpretative aspects. Hence every finding of a regularity on the naturalistic side presents an occasion for inquiry on the interpretative side.

Sometimes it is an occasion that does not lead to much. Some regularities turn out to be the effect of natural causes operating without human design. Famine, following upon certain natural causes like bad weather or shifts in ocean currents, is an example. People regularly perish when their food supply runs out. In the presence of certain causes they are regularly incapable of preventing this from happening. One might wonder whether regularities like these properly belong to social science at all. Are they social phenomena when they operate regardless of social organization and human choices? We may decide not and still be ready to count as falling within the province of social science causes founded in human biology. Social science can, however, be robustly represented in causal inquiries on the naturalistic side without having to carry those inquiries back to biological questions. Moreover, the biological questions come into social science only by way of affecting social organization and human choices.

Some questions for interpretative inquiry arise even in respect to matters that may after inquiry turn out not to be social phenomena at all. For whether or not an instance of famine is an instance of a regularity that human beings do nothing to establish has to be established by interpretative inquiry. Did the famine occur because of human neglect? Because of inadequate institutions, the rules of which failed to require timely precautions? Did the rules actually obstruct remedies, for example, by making witchetty grubs taboo, when people could have sustained life by eating them? Thus it is always relevant when confronted with a regularity about human beings to ask how far it depends on human choices and actions or on human failures to choose and act. Moreover, to speak conservatively, in by far the majority of cases of regularities of interest to naturalistic social science, the dependence exists, and operates, engaging the interest of interpretative social science in a variety of ways at once.

Sometimes the regularity is an intended consequence of acting by a certain rule. Thus a government in Canada stays in office so long as it has been formed by a party with a majority in Parliament that continues to vote cohesively in its support. The rule, which calls for conformity by a group (the party), is that the party must vote cohesively. I am not speaking here of the rule that the government must resign if it loses a vote in Parliament. That rule, a direct counterpart of the regularity that the government resigns when it loses a vote, is certainly an interpretative aspect of the regularity. However, I am deferring discussion of direct counterparts until the next chapter. Even so, the present case requires mention of another rule besides the rule of cohesiveness for the group. For that the government stays in office is an intended consequence cannot be fully explained without considering the intentions of individual members of the party. Each one of them is acting by a further rule requiring individual members to vote with the government. Each intends to vote by that rule. Moreover, each intends by voting by that rule to enable the government to stay in office.

As an intended consequence of actions, a regularity may also depend on the intentions with which people in a position to introduce a new rule bring it into being. A simple case is one in which a government intends to raise the amount of voluntary contributions to political parties. Suppose it introduces a rule under which such contributions are allowed as credits against the personal income tax. This amounts, of course, to modifying the prescription as to what is to be paid in taxes. If the modification has the consequence intended, the taxpayers go along, themselves acting with the intention of increasing with their own contributions the amounts of contributions going to the parties. Governments are always modifying prescriptions about taxes with the intention of achieving certain consequences, however. The intentions of the people subject to the prescription do not always run hand in hand with the intentions of the government. A government may impose taxes on oil companies with the intention of having them pay for the costs of polluting the atmosphere with various lead derivatives and other noxious substances. If the companies pay, it might well be questionable whether they did so with the intention on the part of their executives to reimburse the government and the public for those costs. Would they not be acting simply with the intention of conforming to the rule that such taxes were to be paid and of escaping, with this conformity, the penalties, under the rule, for not paying?

The relation of regularities to matters like intentions and rules is, as one would perhaps expect, even more complicated when the regularities are unintended consequences of human actions or omissions. As I have remarked already, it is under the heading of unintended consequences that the main allowance for naturalistic social science comes from those champions of interpretative or of critical social science who are prepared to make any significant allowance at all. It is also a category of issues that Popper, as a champion of naturalistic social science, regards as setting the social sciences their "main task."[9] Suppose we concede, as we often must, that a certain regularity, however it comes about, does not come about because people intend to have it occur. In particular, it cannot then be a result sought under any rule, whether a rule to which only a group can conform or a rule applying to persons.

It may nonetheless be expected to have a variety of connections with rules and other matters of interest to interpretative social science. In all these connections naturalistic social science, with the regularity, presents interpretative social science with work to do. For example, a consequence—an unintended consequence—of introducing a tax credit for political contributions might be that the distinction between the major parties and minor parties in respect to source of contributions becomes more drastic than ever. Major parties might become more dependent than ever on a few large contributions while minor parties succeed in collecting contributions from supporters who expressly join the parties as members. One aspect of this outcome of special interest to interpretative social science might be that the supporters of the minor parties would in much greater proportion accept the rule that if they supported the parties they should join as dues-paying members. If so, do they not look upon the tax credit differently from supporters of the major parties?

The attempt to get the oil companies to pay for the costs of pollution might also have an unintended consequence, indeed, quite the opposite of the consequence intended. For the oil companies might be able to shift the burden of the tax onto its customers by having them pay higher prices

[9]Karl R. Popper, *The Open Society and Its Enemies,* 3rd ed. (London: Routledge, 1957), 2:95.

for gasoline. This would be the case if the demand for gasoline was relatively inelastic, as economists would say, meaning insensitive to changes in prices. This in turn would be an effect of the consumers' feeling that they had no alternative to buying gasoline in the same quantities as before because they had no alternative to using their cars as much as before. Various rules might lead them to feel this way, among them a settled social rule according to which they could maintain their social status only by having cars. Alternatively, but just the same a matter for the attention of interpretative social science, the consumers might have in parallel so many personal rules, under which keeping and using their cars was a high priority in their budgets, even if there were not sanctions like loss of status to fear.

Parallel personal rules of this sort come into the picture (one might think, come in most plausibly) when the regularity falls in with the common example of an unintended consequence that can be found in the price and demand relation. If the price of a good falls, in certain circumstances, more of the good will be bought. How could this happen except by a lot of consumers deciding to buy more? But each of those consumers makes the decision separately, for herself, and none of them intends that the total amount bought should rise, much less that the total amounts bought of alternative goods should diminish. In other circumstances, if the price of a good falls, less of it will be bought. That is paradoxical, but it is the case when consumers expect, perhaps from hearing that there has been a glut on the supply side, that the price is going to fall further. Again, however, no consumer, in making her own decision, intends to reduce the total amount bought. She is in no position to intend anything of the sort, unlike the people, coordinated by their membership in a party, who intend to add their contributions to others and thereby increase the total going to the party. She decides by her own rule for her own budget.

Yet inevitably, what individual consumers do in these two cases will fall under settled social rules about prudent conduct. At the very least, no one wants to be taken for a fool. Hence people try not to be flagrantly imprudent, mindful to some degree of the sanctions attaching to the rules about prudence. Ridicule is the most common sanction, perhaps, but there are others, ranging from withdrawal of credit and confidence to taking away a person's power to manage his own affairs. At any rate, it is a matter for interpretative inquiry how far the individual actions underlying regularities of supply and demand conform merely to personal rules or come about under the "normative pressure" of settled social ones.

Some regularities depend on differences between people in the sets of rules that they understand well enough to follow. Data on the effectiveness of citizens' groups organized to promote measures of desegregation in American schools or to monitor the operation of such measures once adopted show that when they are effective at all, it is in transmitting influence by the white members of the groups rather than influence by the black members.[10] This is a regularity, established as such by comparing expressions of preference collected from white members and black members respectively with expressions of preference (including policy choices) by government leaders. It is founded on whites' being more active, knowing better how to get access to government leaders, being more familiar with various government programs, being more likely to contact officials, as well as having more money to contribute to politics. In short, the whites know the relevant rules, while the blacks do not; so the blacks, by and large, do not know how to act effectively in these connections. Tally, in an especially memorable passage, which does no discredit to his acute intelligence, tells how uncomfortable and left out he felt at the law court, standing by while Liebow discussed matters with a lawyer: "I didn't even know what you was talking about."[11]

It is often essential to enter into interpretative social science and consider rules just to finish the naturalistic work of establishing causation and the direction of causation. Evidence shows that when plans for desegregating schools are worked out locally there are fewer "serious disruptions" and that "business leaders, white parents, teachers and school boards all began and ended the desegregation process more supportive of local intervention than of federal intervention."[12] But what is the direction of causation? Are the disruptions fewer because the intervenors are local? Or do local officials act only in districts where they can expect "high support and low resistance"?[13] Social scientists who take up these questions would be derelict in their efforts if they did not sooner or later inquire whether there are commonly rules according to which local leaders are heeded while outsiders are defied whenever possible. Note, too, that any inquiry into the degree to which officials expect support or resistance quickly becomes engaged with interpretative questions about how the officials understand the actions that they may do or omit to do and how they think their constituents will understand those actions.

The variety of examples that I have brought up of the interpretative inquiries that may be set afoot by findings, on the naturalistic side of social science, of causal regularities (or candidates for being regularities) should suffice to show how difficult it would be to produce an example of a regularity about which no interpretative questions at all arose. The hypothesis that no such example will in fact be forthcoming thus looks pretty safe from falsification. Even if this safety should prove illusory, it is certainly

[10]Jennifer L. Hochschild, *The New American Dilemma* (New Haven: Yale University Press, 1984), 103–105.

[11]Liebow, *Tally's Corner*, 62.

[12]Hochschild, *Dilemma*, 125.

[13]Questions that Hochschild raises, ibid.

true that causal regularities on the naturalistic side are very commonly capable of raising questions for the interpretative side. However, I do not mean to retreat to this more modest claim unless I am compelled to. I stand, at the end of this chapter, with this universally quantified double hypothesis: All regularities about social phenomena are capable of starting up interpretative inquiries on some line or other. Likewise, all settled social rules are capable of starting up various naturalistic inquiries into their causal aspects. I move on, in the next chapter, to demonstrate an even stronger measure of complementarity. In respect to the phenomena that are the proper subject matter of social science, the key ideas of the two sides are mutually presupposing. It is conceptually impossible to deny the pertinence of mounting, upon the findings characteristic of either side, inquiries characteristic of the other.

# CHAPTER SIX

# Mutual Presupposition

The evidence of mutual support and stimulation already brought up suggests that the naturalistic and interpretative sides of social science are not two separate territories but rather two different entrances to one continuous field of inquiry. But there is more to say. In this chapter, I bring forward a further consideration, which I think should suffice to make the case for unity even with those not already persuaded. The key idea of one side presupposes the key idea of the other, and vice versa. Therefore questions raised by one of these ideas inevitably turn directly into questions raised by the other. A given investigator may choose not to pursue the connection systematically. However, the connection is always there. In all its parts, social science is intimately and fundamentally interdependent. Even differences as striking and significant as may exist on occasion between naturalistic and interpretative inquiries must not be made so much of as to obscure this interdependence, which is therefore best spoken of as unity—one cloth, though woven of different textiles and various colors.

## KEY IDEAS OF THE TWO SIDES

The key idea of the interpretative side of social science, the idea of rules, not only coexists with the key idea of the naturalistic side, regularities. In the basic use that social scientists have for it, which is in application to settled social rules, the idea of rules presupposes the idea of regularities. This relation, moreover, runs both ways. The regularities of causal connection that naturalistic social science seeks to observe in sets of persons or in the institutions to which those persons belong presuppose the existence of settled social rules.

As I have all along, I am taking regularities to be causal relations, represented by statements in which the fulfillment of certain conditions is hypothesized to have certain effects. The statements appear in the first instance as reports of statistical association, in their simplest form unqualified reports that whenever the conditions are observed to be fulfilled, certain other things are observed also. Whenever a vote is taken in Parliament, the parties vote cohesively. To become a hypothesis, which treats the observed association as a causal regularity, the report must shoulder the risk that the regularity will sometime or other fail. It may turn out to have been unwarranted to attach to it, as a causal hypothesis does, contrary-to-fact conditionals along with universal quantification ("whenever").

I have been taking, and I am going to go on taking, rules in a narrow sense as amounting to prescriptions or prohibitions to which clear forms of punishment attach as deterrents to deviation. I shall discuss permissive rules only briefly. I shall not discuss variations in sanction, on which some significant distinctions among rules may be founded. I shall again hardly do more than touch upon conventions. There are, as I noted earlier, various kinds of conventions.[1] They may all be distinguished from rules as not having provisions for enforcement. They are adhered to as devices for coordinating different agents' behavior when the agents already desire to be coordinated. However, conventions do tend to gravitate into becoming rules with sanctions attached. Hence we lose less than might be expected by concentrating on rules.

I shall give very little attention to the attitudes that people may adopt toward rules. Hence I shall be leaving out of account many aspects of intentionality, including, along with subtle matters of internalization, the very difference between internalization and fear-induced conformity. Internalization might be represented, in part, as giving oneself a rule about adhering to a settled social rule. However, I shall give rules that a person may give herself further attention only briefly, for a limited purpose, in a passage dealing with other matters. The connections that I shall be concerned with drive right through these matters, I think without prejudice to them. They can be mapped taking into account only some very general features of rules narrowly conceived.

## THE PRESUPPOSITION RELATION

One concept or complex of concepts can be said to presuppose another when every satisfactory philosophical analysis or characterization of the

[1]See above, chapter 3.

first must draw upon the second. This conception of presupposition is too vague, and too rich, to be equated with any one or two simple logical relations. However, it does embrace, among other things, two simple logical relations. One is a relation between definitions and concepts: The concepts by which, as things stand, each side, naturalistic and interpretative, characterizes the facts that it treats cannot be defined without citing concepts from the other side. Naturalistic social science is interested in rates of unemployment. It cannot have such rates without accepting some interpretative account of what it means to have a job. Interpretative social science is interested in whether husbands try to be steady providers. It cannot find whether they do without counting how often they turn up for a job when they have one, and how often they bring home their paychecks. But if when they have a job they continually turn up at the work site, and if having been paid, they time and again bring home their paychecks, regularities emerge that naturalistic social science can cite as such.

The other simple logical relation embraced in presupposition as I conceive it is a relation between statements and truth-conditions. This relation follows from the definitional one. I shall treat it as equally sufficing to establish presupposition without exhausting the richness of that notion. Mutual presupposition between the interpretative and the naturalistic sides of social science is so intimate that the statements on the one side—indeed, the most characteristic statements, which bear the impress of the key idea of that side—presuppose, among their truth-conditions, statements on the other side, which exemplify its key idea. Often these statements are, in a sense that I shall explain, direct counterparts of the statements presupposing them. Added to the multiple evidence cited earlier of complementarity between the two sides and of mutual support, this mutual presupposition between rule-statements and regularity-statements makes, I think, the case for affirming the unity of social science overwhelming.

## FROM RULES TO REGULARITIES

The implication between rules—settled social rules—and regularities is easier to make out than the implication running in the opposite direction. It has, for one thing, more of the advantage of counterparting. One sort of counterparting consists in a settled social rule's leading immediately to a regularity in which the rule itself figures as a cause. Clearly rules can be INUS conditions: Were it not for the existence of the rule against doing so and the sanctions behind it, would not a number of members of the Canadian Parliament cheerfully accept pay as lobbyists (as their British colleagues openly do)? But rules are more then INUS conditions (whenever they are at least that), for human beings bring them into existence and human beings can suppress them.

Furthermore (a curiously neglected fact, which brings into the picture counterparting even fuller and more symmetrical), rules can serve as the backing required to confer lawlike properties upon the major premises of covering law explanations. Consider the following regularity (stated in terms which are also in standard use for expressing rules and may be used here, too, to express a counterpart rule): "Whenever a sitting Member of the Canadian Parliament loses an election, he gives up his seat to the opponent with the largest number of votes." This regularity is something that we could infer from being told that there is a settled social rule expressible in the same terms. The regularity, if not the rule, might reasonably figure in the major premise of a covering law explanation showing why a certain politician is no longer to be seen in Ottawa. Of course, it would be pedantic to spell the explanation out and state the regularity on any real occasion that would call for the explanation. That fact should not be thought to derogate from the reality of the occasions: People in Ottawa may ask, "Why haven't we seen old Dan Tucker recently?" and be reminded, enthymematically, "He lost his seat in the last election."

Might it not be objected to the major premise, overtly expressed or enthymematically hidden, that it describes no more than a coincidence or a simple induction from an arbitrarily limited set of instances? The backing that the regularity has in the rule, of which it is the direct counterpart, stated in the same terms, saves it from any such objection. The intentionality condition sees to that. So also do the conformity and enforcement conditions. This is so even though any theory that has been set forth here may be not a causal theory but a theory about the contents of a rule-structure. With these conditions fulfilled, the premise supports counterfactual conditionals: "If Dan Tucker had not lost the last election, he would not have given up his seat." How much does it matter that (because the Canadian Parliament, something named and singular, is mentioned) the premise is not fully universal? I hold (somewhat heretically) that it does not matter to the question of providing a covering law explanation. It matters the less when we take into account the fact that the premise applies to future cases not yet observed. On that ground, too, it escapes from the charge of being merely a simple induction from enumerated cases. If it is not without qualification universal in scope, it is in principle capable of accommodating infinitely many cases.

A rule could hardly have a fuller or more direct counterpart than a regularity expressed, like the regularity to which it gives backing, in exactly the same words. Certain complications, however, beset counterparting here, and hence beset the thesis of mutual presupposition running from rules to regularities. The chief complication has to do with evidence of conformity. Some degree of conformity—of people acting in accordance with a supposed rule—is indispensable to the case for ascribing the rule to a society as one on which it has in fact settled. If the rule is not a formally legislated one, perhaps not even one previously formulated, the ground for ascribing the rule vanishes if there is no conformity. If the rule is a legislated one, lack of conformity makes it a dead letter and hence not a settled social rule in spite of its presence in the statutes.

It follows immediately, as we have seen, contrary to the views of some champions of interpretative social science, that statistical evidence is relevant, indeed indispensable, to ascriptions of rules. To be sure, people often ascribe rules without going through the motions of counting. They say, without counting instances, that across Canada a candidate who wins a majority of votes in a riding will be considered elected to Parliament. The absence of statistical methods does not imply the irrelevance of statistical evidence. In such cases the evidence is so familiar, and so much a matter of agreement, that no one thinks it worthwhile to gather it anew. The evidence about conformity—about behavior regularly conforming to the rule—must be there nevertheless. Without it, the ascription of the rule would be defeated.

Yet the evidence about conformity that social scientists accept for the existence of a rule often falls a good deal short not only of perfect conformity but even of conformity along with a few exceptions. If the regularity implied by a settled social rule is only the regularity of conformity, it may have too many exceptions to satisfy naturalistic ideas about what regularities should be. Conformity most of the time and enforcement—penalties—most of the rest of the time are typically all that is required to confirm the existence of a settled social rule. But what then is the regularity that corresponds to the rule?

The evidence of enforcement is in a sense even more important than the evidence of conformity, though it cannot supplant the latter. For it distinguishes—and with unlegislated, unformulated rules it may be all that distinguishes—conformity to a rule from parallel habits, like the habits of rising later on weekend mornings. Ordinarily, we may expect to find that at least some of the people who conform to the rule do so in part because they do not wish to suffer the penalties visited upon those who deviate from it. Even if all the people who conformed were doing what they would have done anyway, in the absence of a rule, we may expect everyone, conformer or deviant, to be aware of the penalties for not doing so. Indeed, those who conform (incidentally to doing just what pleases them anyway) may charge themselves with the task of imposing penalties on the people who do not. Suppose, however, that those who conform do just what they would do anyway, without any awareness of penalties that they might suffer or might mete out. Evidence of enforcement may still be forthcoming and suffice to establish a rule. Deviations get negative reactions, which (as with some rules of language and some rules of face-to-face interaction) have much the same effect as penalties deliberately imposed.

I still mean enforcement, not just acting at cross-purposes, which leads

some authors to speak naturally enough of "self-enforcing conventions"—
like stopping for red lights. Indeed, conventions as such, among them
the conventions of language, may be regarded as "self-enforcing" by definition. With a convention, one may expect it to be enough to deter anyone
attentive to his own interest that deviation will put him, perhaps quite
painfully, at cross-purposes with others. However, people are often inattentive, sometimes irrational, sometimes destructive. Stopping for red lights
in fact falls under a strictly enforced rule. Conventions do quickly give
rise to prescriptions or prohibitions, with specific penalties in the way of
fines, reproaches, ostracism.

In relying so much on the enforcement condition, I am not giving the
attention that champions of the interpretative side of social science want
given to the internalization of rules. They hold, I think quite rightly, that
it is normal for people living by settled social rules to take an "inner
view" of them, in which they feel committed personally to conforming to
them and upholding them.[2] Indeed, this inner view enters into the conception that people have of themselves and their characters. They are people
who fulfill family obligations; in their own eyes, that makes an important
difference between them and people who do not. Moreover, even enforcement is normally carried on with an inner view. The people who act to
enforce a rule have made part of themselves the rules according to which
enforcement is carried out.

If I am giving scant attention to these matters, however, I do so without
prejudice. I am leaving open the question why most people most of the
time conform to any given social rule. It may not be because of external
sanctions; or external sanctions may play only a small part, with relatively
few people. It may be because of widespread deep internalization. Yet if
conformity were, abnormally, in some society wholly contingent for everyone upon external sanctions (as it would be in the sort of organized political
society that Thomas Hobbes [1588–1679] argued for), there would still
be rules to conform to.[3] The rules would invite interpretative inquiry. They
would have counterparts in regularities that invited naturalistic inquiry.
My argument for mutual presupposition is simplified, without losing any
of its strength and without begging any questions to the prejudice of interpretative social science, by leaving internalization and the inner view out
of account.

By allowing for rules with vanishingly little evidence that gives them a
footing in people's intentions, I am, as already admitted, stretching the
notion of a settled social rule pretty far. I claim that social scientists themselves may stretch it just as far, to fill out a system of rules, perhaps, or
to draw a striking contrast between different societies. Obviously, stretching
the notion in this way does not weaken the claim that from every settled

[2]H. L. A. Hart, *The Concept of Law* (Oxford: Clarendon Press, 1961), 85–88, 111–114.
[3]Thomas Hobbes, *Leviathan* (London: Crooke, 1651), Part 2.

social rule an observable regularity may be deduced. That there is a regularity in the stretched cases is not in question. Stretching may impair the chances of carrying out the deduction in the opposite direction. I shall deal with that point in due time.

## THE DISJUNCTIVE FORM OF RULES

The practice of social scientists is to formulate prescriptions and prohibitions specifying conditions under which the actions in question are to be done or forborne. Then—informally, aside from the formulas set down— the social scientists allow that there are exceptions and discuss how far exceptions are dealt with by some means or other of enforcement. Von Wright's approach to the logic of norms takes the same line. There is no standard place for penalties, much less any allowance for exceptions, in his formulas.[4]

This, however, is not the only way to formulate rules. If we stick to it—to formulating rules in what we may call their Common Form—we are liable to miss a number of points of importance about rules: an arresting distinction between two sorts of exceptions; a full sense of the contribution that a rule makes to defining possibilities of action; some important aspects of the implication from the existence of a rule to the existence of a regularity.

An alternative formulation (which has been used in logics of norms other than von Wright's) can be found in an irreverent way of looking at the law that I associate with Oliver Wendell Holmes, Jr. (1841–1935).[5] The law, according to this view, does not say, "Don't embezzle!"; it says, "Either don't embezzle or be prepared to spend six years in the cooler." This, of course, is an exaggeration, as it stands, and literally false. We do perfectly naturally and truthfully say that the law forbids embezzlement; and that, moreover, is precisely what the law itself may say: "Such-and-such amounts to embezzlement; and embezzlement is forbidden." Yet the exaggeration makes an illuminating point. The law regarding embezzlement can be formulated either way. The alternative way brings out features of the law that the first, simpler way does not. It is the same with rules. To formulate a rule in its Common Form is standard and convenient practice. However, the same rule can also be formulated in a Disjunctive Form. I say "the

[4]I am referring to the system presented in Georg H. von Wright, *Norm and Action* (London: Routledge, 1963).

[5]Perhaps without good foundation. The irreverence seems apposite. Holmes's teachings in *The Common Law* (London: Macmillan, 1911) and in his *Collected Legal Papers* (New York: Harcourt, Brace, 1921) are compatible with it. In a passage in the latter book (from the address, "The Path of the Law"), 173ff., he comes very close to expressing essentially the view that I associate with him. But not all the way. The view and the irreverence may have been something that I gathered from someone—a teacher or writer—taking a few liberties with Holmes's view.

same rule" because when one ascribes a rule to a society as one of its current settled social rules, one is (even when one is using the Common Form) implying that both forms hold of it.

Just in defining the possibilities of action more explicitly, putting a rule in its Disjunctive Form takes us a stage further in inquiry. For we are prompted to ask, given that the conditions were such that the rule applied, did N conform (to the embedded prescription or prohibition, the rule in its Common Form) or did she lay herself open to punishment? But the Disjunctive Form contributes more than that. Ordinarily, if the rule that N has to do with is a settled social rule, she will be under various sorts of pressure to conform. These pressures, without derogation from their intentional aspects, can be investigated as causes, contrary to what von Wright says.[6] We can inquire, for example, how effective various different measures of enforcement are. The Blackfoot Indians used ridicule. A standard punishment that they imposed was to have an offender listen all night to the other people in the village laughing at him.[7] Is this as causally effective, by any given standard of effectiveness, as more forceful measures? Even the pressure of a person's own conscience can be investigated causally, for one may inquire how early and how deeply a rule has been internalized, and under what system of social training. When the pressure does not work out to conformity, contravening forces will invite causal investigation. What is present in the circumstances that lead some people—by exception, given the prevalence of the rule otherwise—to deviate?

A further virtue of the Disjunctive Form, however, is that it puts us in a position to distinguish sharply between two sorts of exception to the rule. We can thus see the entire strength of the implication from the rule to a corresponding regularity, which is best taken as disjunctive, too. One sort of exception to the rule—strictly speaking, exceptions to the rule expressed in its Common Form—consists of deviations that are regarded as punishable. Suppose they are in fact penalized often enough to justify saying that the rule is enforced. If the rule is translated into its Disjunctive Form—"Either vote with your party or be condemned for making the party look too disunited to govern!"—exceptions in this first category are brought into the rule. They are not exceptions to the Disjunctive Form. Furthermore, now it is more nearly literally correct to hold that a rule of a society corresponds to an observable, counterpart regularity expressed in the same descriptive terms. Either a Member of Parliament conforms—votes with his party—or he is penalized—by being condemned.

The second category of exceptions to a rule embraces those that the people of whose society it is a rule do not regard as punishable. Either they agree in deeming the actions exceptions justified by some additional

[6]Georg H. von Wright, *Explanation and Understanding* (Ithaca, N.Y.: Cornell University Press, 1971), 146–151.

[7]Clark Wissler, *The Social Life of the Blackfoot Indians* (New York: American Museum of Natural History, 1911), 24.

feature of the circumstances not specified in the conditions expressly incorporated in the rule. Or they are so divided on this point that one cannot speak of a prevailing opinion. Here the formulation of the rule, even in the Disjunctive Form, has failed to match the reality. Whoever aimed to capture a feature of the society in the given formulation fell short of spelling out all the conditions to be associated with the rule. That he fell short comes to light when the exceptions do.

These exceptions seem to me to call for the same treatment as the exceptions covered by the *ceteris paribus* clauses of causal laws. They may result, inadvertently, from the errors to be expected with tentative, approximate descriptions. Or they may be deliberately accepted in the interest of having a simplified empirical theory. They are not necessarily, with rules, more numerous in kind or more frequent in occurrence. There have not been— one may reasonably expect that there will never be—any exceptions to the rule that Presidents of the United States must be native citizens. Exceptions of the second category to the rule that one ought to return a friendly greeting when one is in a position to do so must be almost as few, on Tally's Corner or anywhere else. On the other hand, many rules that it is useful to know about, and hence useful to ascribe to a society, do have lots of exceptions. Even in the national legislature of the United States, it is a rule that members divide and vote on party lines. Party loyalty counts for something, and deviations from it are to some extent punished. There are, however, so many exceptions that in upshot the parties in Congress are not very cohesive compared with Canadian ones.

Exceptions of the second category—the exceptions not regarded as punishable—do originate in part from a consideration that does not apply to the *ceteris paribus* clauses in causal laws. Their presence reflects the character that rules have as imperatives, even on their first promulgation, before it is known whether they will be successfully imposed. As St. Thomas among others has pointed out, to try to specify in the formulation of a rule all the cases that will be held to be justified exceptions defeats the principle that to be imperatively efficient the rule must be readily intelligible.[8] Such specifying cannot be done in advance anyway, because not all the exceptions that will be justified can be imagined.

The imperative character of a rule, moreover, so important in shaping the Common Form, is something that the Disjunctive Form shares. It is as much, or more, of an obstacle as disregard of the Disjunctive Form is to accepting the implication from rules to regularities. The imperative character attaches to persisting, settled social rules. But could we not have an imperative—a decree; or a law just promulgated—with as yet no regularity at all to correspond to it? Indeed might we not have to acknowledge

---

[8]St. Thomas Aquinas, *Summa Theologiae*, 1a2ae, Q. 96, Art. 6, at the end, point 3 (in the Blackfriars edition, vol. xxviii, trans. Thomas Gilby [London: Eyre & Spottiswoode, 1966], 141).

that no regularity may ever correspond to it, because it may turn out to be steadily and ubiquitously disobeyed, and disobeyed with impunity? This has been conceded. If we take (as the ordinary use of "rule" permits) rules at the moment of being laid down as such to be included in the rules of the society under study, the implication will fail.

However, I am, as I made plain earlier, not taking "rules" so widely, much less offering a general theory of rules and asserting that from rules regularities of conformity and enforcement are bound to emerge. If they do not emerge, and this is discovered, social scientists will conclude that there is no settled social rule. It is, of course, a matter of definition that I should be using the term "settled social rule" with this consequence. It is not a matter of definition that so used the term refers to a sort of thing that social scientists are persistently preoccupied with.

## FROM REGULARITIES TO RULES

Settled social rules not only imply regularities. Cast in their Disjunctive Form, they imply regularities, about what people do under certain conditions, that correspond point for point with the rules. Even with rules cast in their Common Form, the implication is accompanied by a direct counterpart of this sort, a regularity about conformity, though it is more likely to be one that is excessively exception-ridden. Now I hold that regularities in social phenomena, at least regularities proper to social phenomena, imply the existence of settled social rules. The implication running in this direction, however, has a much more complicated route to travel. Among the complications is the fact that in many cases it does not directly and centrally run from the regularity to a counterpart rule.

Any regular connection between the rate of inflation and the rate of unemployment is a regularity of social phenomena to which no rule corresponds—no rule for persons, no rule for groups. Even regularities that directly embrace the purposeful behavior of individual persons or of groups do not always imply the existence of corresponding rules. When rising early is just a matter of parallel habits, this is the case. It may be the case, too, with voting on party lines. If Members of Parliament regularly vote—an action with a conscious purpose—with their parties, and it is part of their purpose to do so, it does not follow that there is a rule to this effect. The regularity (the regular cohesiveness) might just be the effect of each Member of Parliament's calculating that it is in her own interest to increase the chances of winning for the party to which she belongs. Epstein in fact treats the cohesiveness of the government party mainly on these lines, though one may well doubt whether Members of Parliament are free to vote as they like, without reproach if they deviate.

The implication from regularities to rules does hold, together with direct counterparting for disjunctive regularities, when we have conforming actions (or forbearances) associated with enforcement: penalties for deviance or subversion; perhaps, as well, rewards for conformity. Epstein's treatment of the cohesiveness of opposition parties is an illustration. Members of Parliament in an opposition party either vote with their party or face disapproval by the public (and on that ground if on no other by fellow Members). This disapproval does not actually have to be expressed. Evidence that it would be forthcoming suffices. A Member of Parliament who is thinking of bolting may be observed to be reminded by fellow Members of what is in store for him. The disjunctive regularity and the corresponding rule in Disjunctive Form stand or fall together.

Again, I am using "rule" to cover cases in which the people subject to the rule are not aware of it either as conformers or as enforcers. This suits the usage of social scientists. I do not think that it can be maintained that all regularities do presuppose rules of this description if of no other. It is a regularity involving human beings and their fate or the fate of their groups that groups which run out of food disappear; and a regularity, too, that criminals who literally lose their heads desist thereafter from crime. However, we can set such regularities aside with the comment that no choices of human beings can affect them. What are left are the regularities proper to social phenomena, which do depend on human choices. If human beings chose to act differently, the regularities would break down. All these regularities, even the regularities of parallel habits, do presuppose rules, whether direct correspondence exists or not.

## CURRENT USE OF ACTION-CONCEPTS

As a comment on the current observed character of social science, we may say that the regularities which it has discovered all involve concepts which can be defined only by referring sooner or later to actions under rules. Sometimes the reference is immediate, as it is in expressing an observed regularity according to which, say, if the men on Tally's Corner marry at all, they marry for the first time at an age no less than three years younger than the median age of first marriage for men in the population of the United States as a whole. Marrying is an action that people take under rules. Sometimes the reference is less immediate. If there is a regularity connecting the rate of inflation with the rate of unemployment, it must be granted that neither inflation nor unemployment is an action that any person takes under a rule. Moreover, though unemployment is a condition that persons fall into, one does not necessarily have to do anything according to a rule to be in that condition. Yet neither inflation nor unemployment can be defined without bringing in rules: on the one hand, rules for exchanging goods and setting prices in the course of such exchanges; on the other hand, rules governing jobs and employment, which distinguish people who have employment from people who do not.

## FURTHER FOUNDATION IN ACTIONS

There is a further, supplementary connection with rules that may be asserted for regularities. This connection is not necessary, given what I have just said, to establish current presupposition. It also turns out to be a connection with a certain amount of leakage. Nevertheless it significantly enriches the case for presupposition in this direction. Social regularities, as I shall now proceed to show, cannot have the foundation that they are required to have in the actions of individual persons unless that foundation includes or connects with actions done according to settled social rules. This is a connection that would hold (distinguishing it from the one asserted in the preceding section) even if the regularities in question, far from employing concepts definable by referring to such actions, belonged to a wholly novel social physics. The connection also figures in the requirements that we impose upon the regularities, proper to social phenomena, that we have in hand. With a little leakage, group facts have to have foundations in the actions of individual persons because human choices make a difference to them and human choices are made (almost always) under the categories of action.

This is sufficiently obvious for regularities in the stating of which there is as immediate a reference to actions under rules as the one about marrying early. It is true, too, however, for regularities where the reference is much less immediate. There the regularity must be founded at least in part in actions of persons that are themselves done under settled social rules, or done as instances of merely parallel habits, or done at random. The first of these three sorts of cases, which can be illustrated by the hypothesized regularity (the curve) connecting inflation with unemployment, falls in with the argument at once. Not everything about the regularity can be explained by pointing to people repeatedly conforming to the same settled social rules about setting and accepting prices—when they choose to strike bargains about prices—including prices for labor power. The actions have to combine in a certain way to produce the curve. Nevertheless, the actions and the rules must be present for there to be prices or jobs or people out of work.

The second sort of case is illustrated by the men on Tally's Corner rising late Saturday and Sunday mornings, if we take their rising to be regularity merely of parallel habits. This is harder. However, might we not expect to find that the men were deliberately "sleeping in," taking this to be a privilege that they could exercise on weekends? They conceive of themselves as doing something the significance of which they and others appreciate by distinguishing it from the alternative of having to get up early—to work or to search for work. We may expect to be in the presence of a rule permitting the men to sleep in on Saturday and Sunday mornings if at no other time. I have not hitherto given much attention to permissive rules. I do not want to go into them at any length, here or later, though they do belong to the repertoire of interpretative social science along with prescriptive rules and prohibitions. For present purposes, it will suffice to point out that the existence of a permissive rule implies the existence of prohibitions against interference and prescriptions about penalizing interference when it occurs. Thus the regularity of rising late, even if it is a regularity merely of parallel habits, may be founded on the existence of disjunctive regularities and of rules of the kinds, prescriptions and prohibitions, on which I have been concentrating.

I may note, furthermore, that every regularity of parallel habits will fall somewhere in a dynamic order that tends to convert it into a regularity backed as a counterpart by a full-fledged rule. A regularity of parallel habits may come into being without any attention. It may obtain attention without being associated with any rule, even a permissive one. It may obtain attention and be associated with a permissive rule without itself falling directly under a counterpart prescription or prohibition. But since, among other things, people dislike having their usual practices disturbed, each of these stages tends to develop into the next. The development, moreover, culminates in a stage beyond, which brings in a counterpart prescription or prohibition to back the rule. People will be ridiculed or otherwise punished for getting up early and stirring about.

Finally, there is the sort of case in which we have a nondisjunctive regularity founded on random behavior. Presumably Members of Parliament from time to time have to sign documents. If whenever they were called upon to do so they acted at random in putting their signatures on the page, it would be equally likely that the signature would be anywhere on the page. This would be a regularity more perfectly manifested the longer the series of trials with different documents and different Members of Parliament. Three comments are in order: The regularity is obviously liable to collapse if the people involved adopt a rule according to which the signature is to be written on the dotted line in the space provided. Furthermore, if the people concerned wanted to act at random, and wanted to make sure of doing so, they would have to follow a rule for randomizing behavior. Finally, the random behavior that the regularity rests on, even if it is entirely spontaneous, is something understood as such by contrast to acting under rules or from parallel habits.

Those comments leave some leakage in the supplementary connection. There is leakage in respect both to random behavior and to parallel habits. Neither of them may bring settled social rules with them to the foundation of the nondisjunctive regularities in question. If the random behavior is spontaneous, there may be no settled social rule operating in the emergence of the regularity, not even a rule prohibiting interference. Equally, we may imagine parallel habits occurring without being given the protection of a permissive rule. They may not have been noticed. Noticed or not, no question about interfering with them may have been raised. So we may not, after all, have a settled social rule at the other end of the supplementary connection.

But what does this mean? What does the leakage amount to? It amounts, in the first place, to the possibility of there being some regularities that are not explicable by group facts. More correctly, it amounts to the possibility of there being some regularities whose foundation in actions by individual persons is not a foundation in actions that can be explained by group facts themselves social in origin. In the second place, however, those actions may often—may for the most part—still be explicable as person facts. The actions will have significance lent them in part by socially shared concepts, in part by personal histories which themselves involve such concepts. In the end, some such actions, now to be regarded more properly as mere events, may escape explanation even of this kind. Then either they are to be explained biologically or not explained at all. In neither case do they belong to what social science proper makes explicable. A leakage through which only the inexplicable escapes is not much of a threat to the unity of social science, though it may be a threat to its scope.

## REASONS, INTENTIONS, CHOICES

There are other ideas characteristic of interpretative social science besides the idea of rules. At the bottom of social phenomena, distinguishing them from phenomena natural but not social, are human choices, and with them reasons and intentions. They may shift so as to remove the foundations of any currently settled social rule and of the current regularities that depend on it. When they go, the causal laws in which social science has captured them will go, too. Are these reasons, intentions, and choices phenomena that themselves escape any relation of mutual presupposition? If so, the argument for there being one social science, even though it may already have said enough about mutual presupposition to be convincing, will have to stop with some matters untidily left over.

Choices I shall not discuss separately. They have already been touched upon and will be touched upon again as I discuss reasons and intentions. Here the easy cases are those in which the reasons, and with them the intentions, recur time and time again. Everyone admits that a person may cite the existence of a settled social rule as a reason for doing something, and intend to do it for just that reason. More recalcitrant are cases in which the reasons are nonrecurrent. I propose to argue that nevertheless to give a reason always amounts at least in part to intending one's action to conform to a rule. The rule may not always be a settled social one. When it is not, the relation of the ideas now under consideration to my main argument about rules and regularities is at best an oblique one— an analogy. Nevertheless, all these cases, like the easy ones, connect up with the thesis of mutual presupposition through the idea of rules. I shall not be able to claim this for the cases that are most recalcitrant of all: those in which the intentions are not, and cannot be, made intelligible by reasons. I shall have to write them off—but so will social science, natural- istic or interpretative. They do not damage the thesis of mutual presupposi- tion, which is not intended to reach any further than social science itself.

Before taking up the matters just mentioned, it will be useful to consider, as an intermediate issue that concerns both recurrent and nonrecurrent reasons, the question, much debated by philosophers in recent decades, whether reasons can be causes. In the course of surveying various ways in which causes have to do with rules and rules have to do with causes, we found no obstacle to something's being counted a cause that it has an intentional feature. On the contrary: Rules—prescriptions, prohibitions, and permissions as well—all have more or less rich intentional features, and at their richest these features do not prevent rules from operating as causes, both of individual actions and of the adoption of further rules. Nor do the intentional ingredients of the actions by which rules are commu- nicated, inculcated, and enforced prevent those actions from being causes.

This evidence, favorable to mutual presupposition, does not extend to settling the issue whether reasons can be causes. The room for causal inquiries that the evidence does establish, let it be noticed, suggests that this issue is not so important to social science generally as it has seemed to many. Comparatively little is to be gained for or against the contention that there are no causes for social science to discover (or no causes of the sorts, supposing there are other sorts, that fall under causal laws) by finding that reasons can be causes or that they cannot. They might be held incapable of being. It might be held that having reasons (a more serious candidate) does not furnish in itself any really convincing examples of causes. The mutual presupposing that binds the two sides of social science together so intimately would remain, and with it an abundance of causes, along with complementation and mutual stimulation short of presupposing. The naturalistic side of social science cannot be shut down without mutilating the interpretative side. It is certainly not going to be demolished by finding that reasons cannot serve as causes.

The issue does have a certain importance for psychology even if it is not crucial to social science as a whole. For if reasons or having reasons cannot be causes, then the naturalistic ambitions of psychology regarding individual facts will have to be confined to inquiries into conditioning. The inquiries could not be directly concerned with people acting according to reasons. Even so, microprocesses in which individual agents had reasons, cited reasons, and acted for reasons could continue to be invoked to explain how certain aggregative facts (as in Epstein's account of party discipline in the Canadian Parliament) were caused. Among the reasons might be reasons that cited or implied the existence of rules. The rules would be among the causes of the aggregative facts in question and so would the individual facts of acting according to the rules. In those actions themselves, however, the reasons would not be causes.

Psychology would still have naturalistic explanations to seek and offer as to how citing certain reasons in certain circumstances came to be part of any individual agent's repertoire. Does it nevertheless have to renounce finding causal connections between reasons for acting and the actions carried out? For whatever the issue is worth, I do not think so. Some philosophers, for example, A. I. Melden, have held that reasons could not be causes because reasons for doing an action must link up with the action through a reason for doing an action expressly of that description.[9] I must have decided to vote with my party, or want to vote with my party. Neither of these reasons, it has been held, can be a cause because the action is described in the same terms and must be so described for the link to hold. The link is thus a logical one, which debars it from being a causal connection.

Some philosophers have held, further, that a reason must be identified with a belief or with a statement believed in. In the second case, a reason is not (ontologically) the right sort of thing to be a cause. In the first case, a reason could figure as a condition among the causal conditions of an action, supposing there are such conditions, but it is not an event. These philosophers, using "cause" more narrowly than I have been, hold that if there is no event that causes an action (which is itself an event), an action will not be caused and will not follow upon the causal conditions given, whether beliefs or any other.

In a famous paper, Donald Davidson showed that none of these arguments amount to much.[10] Coming to have a reason, or thinking of a reason, is an event, and hence the right sort of thing to furnish the critical causal condition for another event's following. Changing from not having in mind a want to stay in the House of Commons and vote for my party to having such a want in mind remains, even under this description, a different event from actually voting. The occurrence of the latter does not follow just by logic from the occurrence of the first. Some other event may intervene, a motion to adjourn, for example.

People's intentions in doing actions are often described in ways that

---

[9]A. I. Melden, *Free Action* (London: Routledge, 1961), 52, 146–147, 154.

[10]Donald Davidson, "Actions, Reasons, and Causes," *Journal of Philosophy* 60 (1963): 685–700.

make plain that they have reasons for doing them and at the same time make plain what those reasons are. "He voted with his fellow Liberals to help make sure that the government stayed in power." The reasons in turn often connect with rules. Explaining how voting with one's fellow Liberals helps make sure that the government stays in power requires reference to the rule that a party must give up office if it is defeated on a motion of any importance. Reasons may be (as in this case) recurrent ones. Recurrence is evidence that the actions done for them are done in accordance with rules in which the same terms as express the reasons appear: "A member of the government party ought to help make sure that the government stays in power."

One might discover of an individual agent that when she thought of a certain reason in certain circumstances she would act in a certain way. Perhaps she would not think of it without being reminded. Perhaps she would think of it on her own now and then, though not always, given various cues in the circumstances themselves. Thus she might write to her mother in the Carolinas when some incident on Tally's Corner reminded her of her mother or of an unanswered letter from her mother. Consider answering the question, "What led her to or made her or caused her to write her mother?," by saying, "She remembered that she hadn't answered her mother's latest letter." Is this not near enough to being equivalent to answering the question, "What reasons did she have for writing her mother?" by saying, "She had a letter from her mother that she hadn't answered," for us to treat having the reason as a cause?

The agent's reason in this case must be susceptible of generalization, or else having it would not be a cause. The reasons that an agent has for acting in certain circumstances may be unique in the sense that they may never in fact apply to the agent again. Yet this fact, much stressed in certain quarters,[11] does not establish a difference in this respect between reasons and causes. A man may find a grizzly bear in his tent only once in his lifetime and still have cause to be scared. Similarly, a woman might have reason to write her mother only once in her lifetime: on the sole occasion on which the two were apart for more than a day. Nevertheless, suppose we know that she is familiar with the rule according to which one member of a family owes another a reply if the first member has taken the trouble of writing a friendly letter. Suppose we know further that she is ready to heed the rule. We could then generalize that whenever those circumstances obtained, and she did consequently have a reason to write her mother, she would write.

The fact that the generalization applies only to one agent does not prevent it from being a generalization, though it falls short of being a perfectly

[11]For example, H. L. A. Hart and A. M. Honoré, *Causation in the Law* (Oxford: Clarendon Press, 1959), 52–53.

universal law. So would a generalization over many agents, confined to those belonging to one group or one society or even one particular subset of societies. Without rising to universal laws, psychology could have a lot to say in making just such generalizations about causal connections between reasons (having reasons) and actions.

Are there any perfectly universal laws to propound about reasons? Or short of that, any probabilistic generalizations that apply to all human beings? I expect that some of the latter can be found in respect, for example, to various human needs, defined with sufficient generality so as not to be tied to specific forms of provision. However this may be, I think that there is no universal law of the form, "For all human beings $N$, if $N$ believes he has a reason to do $A$, and an unobstructed opportunity to do $A$, $N$ will do $A$."[12] This statement is, taken one way, false, since frequently people have a reason to do something but do not do it, perhaps because they give more weight to a reason for doing something else. Taken another way, with less than perfect legitimacy, the statement can be read as one about "a conclusive reason to do $A$." One then prepares to hold that any failure of $N$ to do $A$ given an unobstructed opportunity is decisive evidence that he did not believe himself to have a conclusive reason to do $A$. But then the statement is irrefutable and not even a candidate for being a universal causal law.

The rule under which the nonrecurrent reason for writing the mother in the Carolinas falls is not an idiosyncratic one. It is a settled social rule applying to other people as well that one ought to reply to a friendly letter. Some nonrecurrent reasons, however, may connect only with idiosyncratic rules—rules of personal policy. A man may make it a rule for himself never to divulge political information to a gossip columnist but may only once in his life, as a Member of Parliament, have a gossip columnist approach him. Yet idiosyncratic rules, as rules, are still in principle public and social in the sense that whether or not they are being followed is determined by social standards of evidence. The rules in question, besides being idiosyncratic, may sometimes be rules so unlikely to be tested or to persist as to be more notional than real. There may be no prospect of a gossip columnist approaching with political questions. If one did encounter a gossip columnist, one's ideas about how to deal with such columnists might change at once. One's present ideas about how to deal with them may be just an idle fancy, about how one would act in a political career that is not even going to get started. Nevertheless, the notional presence of the rule suffices to connect the most recalcitrant among nonrecurrent reasons, actual or prospective, through the idea of rules to the idea of

---

[12]The case for something of this sort being a universal law is discussed by Paul Churchland in "The Logical Character of Action Explanations," *Philosophical Review* 79, no. 2 (April 1970): 214–236; and by Alexander Rosenberg, in *Sociobiology and the Preemption of Social Science* (Baltimore: The Johns Hopkins University Press, 1980), 95–102.

regularities and the idea of causes. So long as people persist with such rules, the rules enable us to formulate causal regularities for the persons concerned: "Whenever the circumstances are such as to fulfill conditions $C_1$, $C_2$, $C_3$, etc., the agent in question will do $A$."

What we have in these personal rules is an analogue of the point to be made in the argument for social ones. They, like the causal regularities that correspond directly or indirectly to them, are liable to be transitory. It is more than an analogue. If social rules and the causal laws that correspond to them are transitory, it is in part just because the people whose rules are in view are capable of embarking on idiosyncratic rules of their own, which they can choose to abandon in turn. In this we can see some of the depth as well as some of the complication in the potential transitoriness of social regularities.

There are perhaps vestigial cases of reasons for actions in which the above implications, holding even for nonrecurrent reasons, fail. They would be vestigial cases just because of this failure. In these cases, statements by the agents would be accepted as giving reasons for their actions, but they would not be reasons that made the actions intelligible. All that they would do would be to establish that the actions are deliberate. Thus, if someone were asked why he had tried to fry a batch of newts in his hat, and replied, "I just felt like it," we would still be at a loss to understand how the intention originated, but we would know (taking the reply to be true) that the action was done deliberately. Already, if the reply shifts to something like "I was curious to see what would happen," we begin to have a reason of a normal, generalizable sort.

Whether the term "reason" is properly used in the vestigial cases or not, there is no doubt that people can intentionally do extraordinary things. There is no doubt, either, that some of these things escape our powers of explanation. Here, again, we come at the bottom of social phenomena to the fact that people can choose to do things which depart from any hitherto established regularities.

## THE LIMITS OF SOCIAL SCIENCE

We could imagine a society in which everything that everyone did fell simultaneously under a rule, even a nondisjunctive rule, and a regularity. We must regard it as more than a logical possibility that even so those rules and regularities may be unsettled, given the frequency with which rules and regularities can be observed to be unsettled, sooner or later, in other societies. We know as an empirical fact that the possibility of rules and regularities being unsettled is realized to a very significant extent in our own society. It is a persisting, ironic obstacle to the generalizing ambitions of social science, naturalistic, interpretative, or critical, that social science arose as a response to the perplexities created by the breakup, well under way in the eighteenth century, of traditional societies. The old, immemorial rules have been so far unsettled, and successor rules subject to so much shifting, that agents are frequently compelled to create their own terms of social intercourse. They have to negotiate what the rules shall be as much as fall in with given ones.

Even so, the unsettling and shifting often comes about because people are shifting, in response perhaps to changes in technology, to new social rules, or because people are following for reasons of their own idiosyncratic rules rather than social ones. We have in such cases prospects of explanations from both naturalistic and interpretative social science running to the bottom of the phenomena. To the extent that the unsettling and shifting is at bottom to be attributed to intentions, and with them choices, that cannot be made intelligible by reasons, the chances for social science of explaining the changes at issue are diminished. The chances are by no means eliminated: We already have the beginning of a causal generalization when we hold that the changes are due to such intentions and choices. We can hope to specify the conditions under which people resort to such intentions and choices. When we cannot, we do not have to give up the thesis of mutual presupposition, much less the thesis of unity. We simply have to recognize, for the moment at least, a limit to what social science, naturalistic, interpretative, or critical, can do.

# For Further Reading

Besides the works cited in the text, almost all of which are accessible to readers with only so much orientation as this book provides, the following may be mentioned.

For the naturalistic view of social science, see ERNEST NAGEL, *The Structure of Science* (New York: Harcourt Brace, 1961), and the previous book on the philosophy of social science written for the series in which the present one appears: RICHARD S. RUDNER, *Philosophy of Social Science* (Englewood Cliffs, N.J.: 1966).

For the interpretative view, see PETER WINCH, *The Idea of a Social Science* (London: Routledge, 1958), and HILARY PUTNAM, *Meaning and the Moral Sciences* (London: Routledge, 1978). WILLIAM H. DRAY, in *Philosophy of History* (Englewood Cliffs, N.J.: Prentice-Hall, 1964), resists on similar grounds the application of the naturalistic view to research in history. Again more sympathetic to the interpretative view than to the naturalistic one is C. DYKE, *Philosophy of Economics* (Englewood Cliffs, N.J.: Prentice-Hall, 1981).

For the critical view, as embodied in critical social theory, see THOMAS MCCARTHY, *The Critical Theory of Juergen Habermas* (Cambridge, Mass.: MIT Press, 1978), and the historical account given by MARTIN JAY in *Dialectical Imagination* (Boston: Little, Brown, 1973). Sharp criticism of critical social theory can be found in MICHAEL LESSNOFF's contributions to S. C. BROWN, ed., *Philosophical Disputes in the Social Sciences* (Brighton, Sussex: Harvester Press, 1979), 89–116, 140–147.

For the three-sides view taken in the present book as its point of departure, see the landmark article by BRIAN FAY and J. DONALD MOON, "What Would an Adequate Philosophy of Social Science Look Like?," in the journal *Philosophy of Social Science* 7 (1977): 209–227.

On the special topic of scientific explanation, see BAS VAN FRAASSEN, *The Scientific Image* (Oxford: Clarendon Press, 1980), 41–69.

On quantitative thinking in the social sciences, see W. ALLEN WALLIS and HARRY V. ROBERTS, *Statistics: A New Approach* (Glencoe, Ill.: The Free Press, 1956), 3–99, and THOMAS C. SCHELLING, *Micromotives and Microbehavior* (New York: Norton, 1978).

On the case for axiomatization, see GILLES-GASTON GRANGER, *Formal Thought and the Sciences of Man,* trans. Alexander Rosenberg and Carolyn R. Fawcett (Dordrecht, Holland: Reidel, 1983), 117–139.

On the theory of action, closely related to the concerns of the interpretative view, see LAWRENCE DAVIS, *Theory of Action* (Englewood Cliffs, N.J.: Prentice-Hall, 1979).

On the learning of rules by conditioning, see J. F. SCOTT, *Internalization of Norms* (Englewood Cliffs, N.J.: Prentice-Hall, 1971).

Other books on the philosophy of social science that are in my view especially convincing include ROY BHASKAR, *The Possibility of Naturalism* (Brighton, Sussex: Harvester Press, 1979); MICHAEL LESSNOFF, *The Structure of Social Science* (London: Allen & Unwin, 1974); and (for Runciman's own view), W. G. RUNCIMAN, *A Critique of Max Weber's Philosophy of Social Science* (Cambridge: Cambridge University Press, 1972).

The books just mentioned treat much the same problems as the present one. For an illuminating philosophical discussion of a different range of topics, see PAUL DIESING, *Science and Ideology in the Policy Sciences* (New York: Aldine, 1982).

# Acknowledgments

---

Earlier versions of the overall argument of this book figured in papers read at the University of Chicago in February 1983, at the annual meeting of the Canadian Political Science Association in Vancouver, June 1983, and at the annual meeting of the American Political Science Association in Chicago, September 1983. I also rehearsed the argument with a class at Dalhousie in the fall of 1982 and with one at the University of Chicago in the spring quarter of 1984. Let me thank everyone who took part in these discussions. Reflected in specific passages of the present text are the comments of Charles Silver, at the first presentation in Chicago, and of Klaus Amburn and Christopher Drennan, in the class there. Less discernable in effect, perhaps, but still memorably specific were points raised by Matthew Davis, Kathy Daymond, Ian Greig, Jennifer MacLeod, and Donald Westin, in the Dalhousie class. My colleagues in philosophy at Dalhousie have been, as is their wont, usefully provocative, not only in the departmental colloquia in which the themes of the book have come up. Robert Martin, in particular, has had a special impact on my discussion of rules. Jennifer Smith, a Dalhousie colleague in political science, brought Bourdieu's work to my attention. John Cornwall, in economics at Dalhousie, commented on the initial chapters and has held many discussions with me about the current state of economics. Margaret Gilbert, among colleagues farther afield, made some telling and helpful points about the discussion of group facts. Florian Bail, colleague and friend, gave the chapter on critical social theory two rounds of searching criticisms, which led directly to two rounds of improvements on my part. What is judicious in the chapter is as much to his credit as to mine, or more. Brian Fay, Jennifer Hochschild, and Gregory Kavka did me the magnificent favor of reading a whole draft. I have tried to be properly grateful by trying to do justice to their comments. I have tried to do justice, too, to the comments of the publishers' readers, who gave me something to work upon even when (by exception) they seemed to me to be wrong-headed. I am grateful to the editorial staff at Prentice-Hall, to Monroe and Elizabeth Beardsley for encouraging me to write the book, and to Tom Beauchamp for close criticism while it was being written. I owe a debt to Alexander Rosenberg, too, for recent encouragement and for collaboration years ago in writing and teaching in the philosophy of social science. The Government of Canada provided me in the spring and summer of 1985 with an A-plus student research assistant, Mary Gordon, who worked hard and skillfully to complete the documentation for the book. It was she who tracked down the Blackfoot Indians and King Frederick William I. Leslie Adamson and my wife Margaret Odell took pains that I appreciate—round after round of pains in Margaret's case—to see the book through the word processor. For extra secretarial assistance on this and many other projects, I am grateful also to Marlene McAdoo.

Parts of the book reproduce, or run close to reproducing, passages from the paper read to the American Political Science Association and passages from a paper, "The Conditions on Which Rules Exist," forthcoming in the Library of Living Philosophers volume on the philosophy of Georg H. von Wright. I am grateful to the Association and to the editor of the Library respectively for permission to use material from these papers, and grateful to the *Philosophical Review* for permission to use some lines from a book review that I published there in 1978. William Dray helped me a good deal with the paper for the von Wright volume and thus must be thanked as one of the influences on the present book, too.

D.B.

# Index